# THE
# ALNWICK & CORNHILL
# RAILWAY
## Also known as the
# ALNWICK & COLDSTREAM

## *John Addyman and John Mallon*

### *With contributions from Vera Mallon and Chris Woolstenholmes*

**NORTH EASTERN RAILWAY ASSOCIATION**

Published by the North Eastern Railway Association, September 2007. Reprinted August 2008

ISBN 978 1 873513 65 1 Paper bound edition
ISBN 978 1 873513 70 5 Case bound edition

Layout by John Addyman

Printed in Great Britain by The Amadeus Press Ltd.

# THE NORTH EASTERN RAILWAY ASSOCIATION

Formed in 1961, the NERA caters for all interested in the railways of north-east England, in particular the North Eastern Railway and the Hull & Barnsley Railway, from their early history down to the present day. This also extends to the many industrial and smaller railways that operated alongside them. Interests range over all aspects of development, operation and infrastructure of the railway, including such diverse activities as locomotive history, rolling stock, train services, architecture, signalling, shipping, road vehicles and staff matters – both for the general enthusiast and model maker.

With in excess of 700 members, regular meetings are held in York, Darlington, Hull, Leeds and London. A programme of outdoor visits, tours and walks is also arranged. There is also an extensive library of books, documents, photographs and drawings.

Members receive a quarterly illustrated journal, the NORTH EASTERN EXPRESS, and a newsletter, covering membership topics, forthcoming meetings and events in the region together with book reviews and a bibliography of recent articles of interest. Over 180 issues of the EXPRESS have been published to date.

The Association also markets an extensive range of facsimiles of NER documents, including diagram books. timetables and other booklets from original NER material while it is developing an expanding range of original publications, available to members at discounted prices.

A Membership Prospectus can be obtained from the Membership Secretary:
Mr. T. Morrell, 8 Prunus Avenue, Kingston Road, Willerby, Hull, HU10 6PH.

A sales list of other NERA publications can be obtained from the Sales Officer:
Mrs. C. E. Williamson, 31 Moreton Avenue, Stretford, Manchester, M32 8BP.
(PLEASE ENCLOSE A STAMPED ADDRESSED 9" X 4" ENVELOPE WITH YOUR ENQUIRIES).

*Front cover: Edlingham Viaduct seen from above Edlingham station as it might have appeared in the late 1920s with class D17 No. 1621 hauling the two diagram 145 coaches allocated to the branch. Painting by David Sutcliffe.*
*Title page illustration: the start of the branch with the old and new signal cabins at Alnwick taken just prior to its opening to passengers in September 1887. Note that the signal lamps and spectacles are fixed some distance below the signal arms. NERA.*

# CONTENTS

## INTRODUCTION AND ACKNOWLEDGEMENTS

The Alnwick and Cornhill (A&C), or Alnwick and Coldstream line was one of those railways that was built to serve the social needs of a sparsely populated area, almost as an obligation, by a large, rich railway company. The passenger service was axed as early as 1930, after a life of 43 years. Its route follows close to the main roads of the district, and its still extant, elegant station buildings, set in beautiful countryside, have retained an interest in the line long after its closure.

John Mallon (1932-2002) was born in Alnwick after the passenger service was withdrawn, but he formed a life-long interest in the line. If this history 'reaches places that have never been reached before' it is due to John's research over a period of 50 years. Working as a clerk on the line during the early years of his railway career allowed him access to information that usually disappeared with the closure of a branch. He was also able to talk to many people who had worked or travelled on the line, and to make his own footplate journeys on the remaining goods services. He conscientiously recorded most of the information that he had gleaned with the intention of us jointly producing this book. Although we wrote an article, which appeared in *Back Track* in November 1991, ill-health prevented him from completing his input for this book. However, it is appropriate that he is credited again as joint-author.

My interest in the line commenced in the 1960s, when I followed its route whilst on holiday in Northumberland. I was allowed to make copies of some of the station drawings, when working for BR at York. When these were used in the North Eastern Railway Association's *Express,* John told me of his interest in the line, and we decided to work together on its history. Some research to complement John's was carried out by my son David and me in Northumberland County Archives. Since John's death his sister, Vera, has taken up local research in Alnwick, and has come up with even more valuable background information. Visits to the National Archives (PRO), at Kew, by Bill Fawcett and me have filled in further gaps. Bill has provided constructive criticism and made many helpful suggestions during the preparation of this book. Chris Woolstenholmes has kindly sorted out the signalling details.

When John gave me the commercial information that he had obtained he had not analysed it, and failed to appreciate that the A&C never made a profit. The operating and maintenance costs always exceeded the meagre returns from the traffic. The declining fortunes of rural branch lines, after the coming of the motor vehicle, were something that nineteenth century railway promoters could not have foreseen. Later, even the senior managers of the nation's railways, prior to Beeching, seemed to be blind to the burgeoning losses made by these lines. Although this was a real bonus for the few remaining users and for railway enthusiasts it was not so for the shareholders and, later, the taxpayer. Sadly, the story that will unfold is one that shares many parallels with rural lines throughout Britain – it would have been a lot nicer to record a roaring success.

John Mallon had a huge collection of photographs of the line but, unfortunately, it does not include a lot of pictures of the trains. As passenger trains were withdrawn in 1930 photographs of them working on the line are very rare. However, David Sutcliffe's painting on the front cover recreates a scene as it may have appeared in the late 1920s. Shots of the parcels trains are confined to the last days of their operation on the south end of the line and there are no pictures of heavy cattle trains struggling up to Summit to enliven the pages. A number of the photos do not have any information as to location, date, photographer or copyright holder. Photos without provenance have therefore been credited to the J. F. Mallon collection.

John Addyman

## CHAPTER ONE: EARLY RAILWAY DEVELOPMENTS

The largest part of Northumberland, which lies a little north of the main Tyne Valley and west of the Newcastle and Berwick main line, was, for want of a better name, called Central Northumberland by the railway promoters. It is very sparsely populated, but as early as 1850 the only places of any size not reasonably served by the Newcastle & Berwick and Newcastle & Carlisle railway companies were Wooler, Rothbury and Bellingham. The rest of the population was scattered in a number of small villages, hamlets and isolated farms. The census of 1851 gave a figure of less than 10,000 inhabitants for the area excluding the towns. Because there was negligible mineral exploitation, no industry and a reduction in arable farming the numbers had been declining with migrations into the Tyneside and Wearside industrial areas since the early 19th century. The question of providing further railways for such a district with a reasonable hope of financial success was somewhat difficult. Surprisingly, by grouping (1923) the area had a network of 140 miles of North British (NBR) and North Eastern Railway (NER) branch lines. Oddly, the Scottish company's lines were to the south of the district and the NER's mainly to the north.

When railways were first built it was out of necessity based on a fair economic case, but soon rivalry and prestige, without any real consideration of commercial success, were also reasons for promoting them. Later, the benevolence of a large, rich company could provide transport in a remote district of its territory with little chance of a financial return on the capital expended. The railways in the area under consideration appeared for all these reasons.

The earliest two branches built in the area were authorised under the Newcastle & Berwick Act of 1845. The first, from Tweedmouth to Sprouston, was completed in 1849.[1] It was linked to the NBR line through Kelso two years later to provide the only southern rail outlet from the central Borders until the Waverley route (Border Union Railway) was completed, to Carlisle, in 1862. The other branch authorised under the Newcastle & Berwick Act was the three-mile spur from Lesbury to serve Alnwick; it opened in 1850. The Alnwick and Cornhill (A&C), the subject of this book, was eventually to provide an inland link between these two branches.

When petitioning for Alnwick to be served by the proposed Newcastle & Berwick main line in 1844 the residents included this description of their town: -

> 'It is the County Town of Northumberland, where the County Court of the Sheriff is heard monthly, and the Quarter Sessions of the peace once a year. The population of the parish is 6,636, and the gross estimated rental on which the poor rate assessment is made amounts to £32,000 per annum. It has a weekly market for corn, provisions and other articles; the quantity of grain sold having amounted in some years from 50,000 to 70,000 quarters, producing from £100,000 to £140,000. There are three principal Fairs for Cattle, Sheep and Horses, and for general merchandise, held in the Town during the year, besides large markets for hirings. The Mail and four other stage Coaches pass north and south daily; between fifty and sixty carriers attend the weekly market, and a considerable number on other days. Several extensive concerns are carried on in the Town. There are four Bank Agencies, several wholesale and retail Grocers, Drapers, Wine and Spirit Merchants, Brewers and Maltsters, Tanners and Leather Dressers, besides an Iron Foundry, a Coach Manufactory, and other establishments of respectability.'

William Weaver Tomlinson gives more prosaic descriptions when writing in his other book, *Comprehensive Guide to Northumberland*, at the time that the A&C was being built: -

> 'Alnwick [the seat of the Dukes of Northumberland] ranks next to Newcastle among the Northumbrian towns, both in regard to size and importance, but, unlike the great capital of the coal district, it has remained unaffected by the tremendous industrial changes of the century. Lying peacefully amid its pastoral hills, by the side of a river unpolluted by modern commerce, this ancient Border town still presents the plain and austere aspect which it wore when the great stage coaches passed through on their way from London to Edinburgh.'[2]

'Wooler, the capital of this hilly district [the Cheviots], is a quiet and small rural town, with little of the picturesque about it, delightfully situated on a slope above the Wooler water. The houses are plain and unattractive, few possessing gardens in front.' [3]

Cornhill was described as 'a small agricultural village of a single street, situated, as the name implies, in the midst of rich corn lands.' A mile away, on the north side of the River Tweed, the Scottish town of Coldstream is reached by John Smeaton's magnificent road bridge of 1766.

Most of the A&C would not have been required if an earlier proposal by a Mr. Remington had been pursued. This 104 mile long line from Newcastle to Dalkeith via Morpeth, Whittingham, Wooler, Kilham and Kelso was under consideration by the Smith-Barlow report for the Board of Trade in 1840. The engineering works would have been extremely heavy with deep cuttings, huge embankments and two tunnels: one at least two miles long was needed under Rimside Moor, near Edlingham, and another of five miles was required under Soutra Hill to get to Dalkeith. [4]

However, the first practical proposal for a main line from Newcastle to Edinburgh via Berwick was deposited on 1 March 1839. It was the Great North British Railway with Thomas Grainger and John Miller as engineers for the Scottish end and George and Robert Stephenson for the rest. The line was generally to the east of the present main line, and a lot better aligned. There was no branch to Alnwick, and Morpeth was to be served by one almost five miles long. [5] Miller went on to build the north end of the line from Edinburgh to Berwick, but the English end ran into difficulties with a major landowner when it was proposed to pass between Howick Hall (NU 248175) and the coast, just north of Alnmouth. Robert Stephenson modified the alignment to serve Morpeth and to cross the River Aln west of Lesbury (NU 229121), but this dispute gave I. K. Brunel a chance to promote his atmospheric railway as an alternative from Newcastle to Berwick. Although it was backed by Lord Howick and several local M.Ps, Brunel's line lost the fight and was formally withdrawn on 28 June 1845. The Newcastle and Berwick Act was given the royal assent on 31 July 1845. [6]

An abortive main-line proposal of 1845 was the Newcastle, Edinburgh and Direct Glasgow Railway routed via Ponteland and Carter Bar to Edinburgh, with branches to Hexham and Bellingham. In 1852 and 1853 railways were projected from Acklington, on the main line, along the Coquet Valley to Rothbury, and from Morpeth to Kelso via Rothbury, Whittingham and Wooler, but nothing came of them (fig. 1.2). [7]

In the mid-nineteenth century how could the centre of Northumberland best be served? The proposal from Acklington to Rothbury plus a spur off the Kelso branch to Wooler would have served the two largest towns with the construction of less than 25 miles of railway at an expenditure of about £170,000; the Morpeth to Kelso would have cost around £500,000 for nearly 60 miles of railway. A third possibility, for a route from Newcastle via Ponteland, Rothbury and Wooler to Kelso, over 75 miles long, would have needed an investment of well over £700,000 at that time. [8] As we shall see, the strategy that was to emerge was not to serve the population as economically as possible, but to beat rivals either real or imaginary.

The NER was formed in 1854 by a merger, and its directors still had painful memories of the Hudson debacle of 1849 so their approach to new railway construction, especially in rural areas, was initially extremely cautious. Their policy, and the folly of not observing it, was recounted by their chief engineer, Thomas Elliot Harrison (1808-1888), in a discussion at the Institution of Civil Engineers in 1867: -

'In a purely agricultural district without either manufacturers or mineral productions, the cost of what the line ought to be, to make the traffic pay, was of a very simple kind. He was satisfied that the results of the actual traffic to be produced from any line of that nature were not more than £7 to £10 per mile per week; and he took that traffic return as a basis of what cost the line ought to be, which, to pay 5 per cent, and with 50 per cent for working expenses, ought not to exceed £3,000 to £5,000 per mile. Generally speaking, in this country the mistake was made at the commencement. Instead of estimating what the country was likely to produce, and then saying, unless the line could be constructed for a certain price it would not pay 5 per cent, lines were laid out without regard to the question whether the traffic was likely to pay or not. He was satisfied, if promoters were to take a more commercial view of the matter, and if the lines were constructed only at such a cost as to afford reasonable prospects of the traffic giving a fair return upon the capital, there would be found even at this time, abundance of people ready to invest their money; but when a line was made at a cost commensurate with traffic of £20 per mile per week, whilst only producing £10 then, he thought, people would be acting an insane part to put their money into it.' [9]

The NBR, the other contender for rural Northumberland, was prepared to shoot off in any direction without regard for viability. The board's policy was summed up by its chairman, Richard Hodgson (1812-1877)[10], when addressing the shareholders at their half-yearly meeting in Edinburgh on 24 March 1859. He said: -

'Had they (the NBR) been shut up in Hawick by the Caledonian and by the NER at Kelso and Berwick…in what position would they have been? They would have been totally dependent on these companies, and it was the duty of the directors of these companies to bring the screw on the North British, and to have made its interests subservient to their own interests. He would have done so himself had he been a director of these companies.' [11]

# DEDICATION.

## TO THE

## MERCHANTS AND COMMERCIAL CLASSES

### INTERESTED IN THE TRADE OF

## NEWCASTLE,

### AND TO THE

## OWNERS OF PROPERTY IN THE VICINITY,

This Pamphlet — being an attempt to show what are their true interests in the Railway struggles now impending—

Is respectfully dedicated

By their obedient Servant,

## J. BAXTER LANGLEY.

Figure 1.1: cover of a pamphlet issued about the evils of North British Railway aggression in 1861.

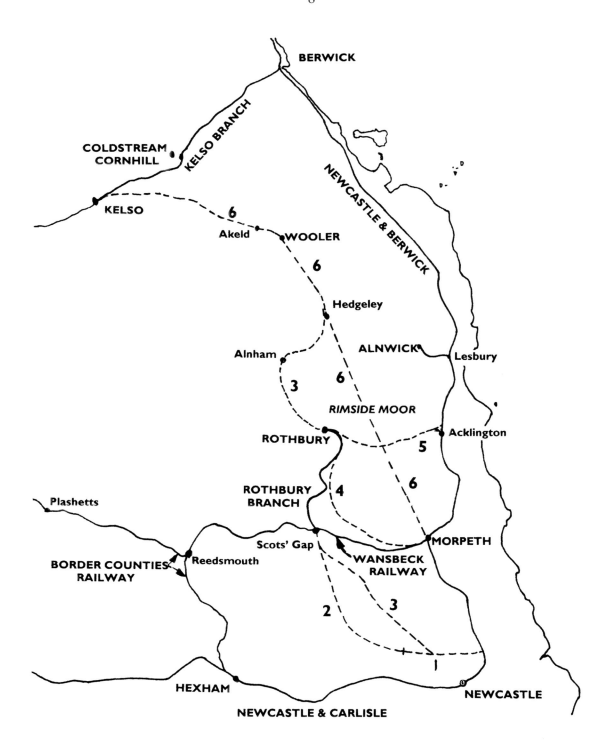

**Figure 1.2: a map showing some of the railways built and projected in the area bounded by the Scottish border, the Newcastle & Berwick and the Newcastle & Carlisle railways between 1840 and 1880. The projected lines, shown dotted, are: 1 the Blyth & Tyne Walbottle Branch, 2 the South Northumberland Railway, 3 the Northumberland Central Railway, 4 the Morpeth & Rothbury Railway, 5, the Acklington & Rothbury Railway, 6 Remington's Morpeth & Dalkeith Railway, which shared common ground with the central section of the Alnwick & Cornhill and Northumberland Central. The map of the Alnwick & Cornhill appears as figure 3.2. The Newcastle & Berwick underwent several substantial modifications before the final route was established in 1845. J. F. Addyman.**

The NER had made no attempt to 'bring the screw' on the NBR, and, in fact, the previous year had seen both companies starting serious negotiations for their merger. However, the proposed division of joint profits of 83% to 17%, based on performance in favour of the NER, was not palatable to the NBR shareholders; in spite of the NER's offers of concessions the negotiations closed in 1859. The division of profits indicated, to a large extent, the validity of the NER's more cautious policies.[12] If the merger had taken place railway development in rural Northumberland would have taken a very different course.

In July 1854 a railway was authorised that was to give the NBR its first toehold in Northumberland, and was also to form the first link in a chain of events that would eventually lead to the building of the Alnwick and Cornhill railway. This line was the initially independent Border Counties Railway, which left the Newcastle & Carlisle Railway (N&C) just west of Hexham to serve the North Tyne valley and a grossly overrated coalfield at Plashetts (now partly submerged under Kielder Water). The line was amalgamated with the NBR on 13 August 1860 when it had only completed the first 11 miles from Hexham to Wark.[13] It was extended into Scotland, with a total length of 40 miles, to meet the Border Union Railway (BUR) at Riccarton Junction. It was opened throughout simultaneously with the southern end of the BUR (Waverley route) in 1862.

The engineer for the BUR and Border Counties Railways was John Furness Tone (1822-1881). He was also the engineer for the Blyth and Tyne and lessee of Plashetts Colliery. He worked with Richard Hodgson on several projects for the NBR; the most ambitious being the first proposal for a bridge over the Firth of Forth in 1862.[14]

In October 1858 the Wansbeck Railway was projected from Morpeth to join the Border Counties at Reedsmouth Junction, a distance of 28 miles, with J. F. Tone as engineer. Although it was opposed by the NER it was authorised on 8 August 1859. It was opened from Morpeth to Scots' Gap in 1862, incorporated in the NBR on 21 July 1863, and completed to join up with the Border Counties line in 1865. This railway, which had no passenger or freight potential, was seen by some as an ambitious, and totally unnecessary, plot by the NBR and its allies to acquire a route independent of the NER from Newcastle to Edinburgh.[15] The Blyth & Tyne Railway (B&T), which was building a terminus near the centre of Newcastle, was on much more friendly terms with the NBR than the NER at this time (although the B&T was to be vested in the NER in 1874). With the aid of the B&T to give the NBR access from Morpeth to Newcastle it was possible by a very slow and circuitous route (138 miles) to reach Edinburgh by using the Wansbeck, Border Counties and Waverley lines. However, in 1862 the NBR had already achieved another route into Newcastle over the Newcastle and Carlisle, which had just become part of the NER system.

Originally, the NBR had done its best to defeat the Bill for the NER and N&C merger, and it was not until 1862 that its opposition was withdrawn with a condition that the NER gave running powers for all traffic from the Border Counties line over the 22 miles from its junction, west of Hexham, to Newcastle.[16] This arrangement was later to cost the NBR dearly as in return the wily NER secured running powers for coaching traffic only from Berwick to Edinburgh and by 1890 it had ousted the NBR from running any expresses over its own main line. The NBR had conceded rather a lot for nothing as, within a year, the Border Counties could only sustain two passenger trains a day in each direction. In spite of the fact that it now had an alternative route from Newcastle to Edinburgh that was only four miles longer than the East Coast main line the idea of through services was never pursued.

Having got this far, why did the NBR chairman and his allies put their weight behind another dubious railway project in the autumn of 1862? This proposal was called the Northumberland Central Railway (NCR), and it was authorised on 28 July 1863 to be built from Scots' Gap to Cornhill on the NER's Kelso branch. At this time they could have cut their losses by not completing the remote 14 mile section of the Wansbeck line from Scots' Gap to Reedsmouth, and instead they could have built either the 13 mile southern end of the NCR as far as Rothbury or the potentially more profitable and better supported northern end from Cornhill to Wooler – with the option of joining them up later.

John Thomas, in *The North British Railway* (1969), has suggested that its lines were a means by which Richard Hodgson (the NBR chairman and director of the NCR) in his other role as an M.P. for Tyneside sought to please his electorate.[17] It could also be argued that the lines were a result of his obsession not to be 'shut up' by other companies in his attempts to link Edinburgh and Eastern Scotland with the industrial areas of Northern England. In order to reach this goal expense seemed to be no object. Under his chairmanship, in 1860 and 1861, the NBR together with the London & North Western Railway had pledged two-thirds of the capital for a very nearly successful attempt to gain authorisation for a new route to reach Tyneside from Lancashire. This was to use the South Durham and Lancashire Union Railway over Stainmore, and more than 60 miles of very steeply graded new single-line railway to reach Newcastle. Surely, the NER did the promoters a favour when it managed, at a last ditch attempt, to get the Bill thrown out from the House of Lords.[18] How could the NBR afford to finance it? It could not and, in the early 1860s, it became necessary to falsify its accounts to declare any dividend. When Lord Redesdale was chairman of a Select Committee, into an unrelated NBR merger in 1862, he summed up by saying: 'The North British are the best hands in the world that I know for making bad bargains'!

It was partly major railway politics and partly local canvassing that provoked a flicker of NER interest in rural Northumberland, and its look at a line from Alnwick to the Kelso branch. On 4 November 1844 a railway committee had been set up in Alnwick 'to defeat any attempt that may be made to carry the [Newcastle & Berwick] railway at a distance from the town.' The Duke of Northumberland was quite happy for railways to avoid the town. However, with the support of Lord Dalhousie, then President of the Board of Trade, the committee partly succeeded in its aim by getting a three-mile branch from the main line to the town added to Robert Stephenson's Newcastle & Berwick Railway Bill in January 1845.[19]

Spurred on by this earlier success, another committee in Alnwick had become intent, in the late 1850s, on improving the transport links with the area to the north west at least as far as Wooler. By December 1859 they had even worked out, in some detail, the start of a route for a railway to Wooler. It was obvious to them that the line would have to avoid the Duke's prime parkland (Hulne Park), and start with a more circuitous and difficult alignment to the south west of Alnwick. John Thompson, the town's surveyor, had suggested some more easily graded lines, than that later chosen by the NER, by having a tunnel more than a mile long under Alnwick Moor.[20] By early 1860 the whole route from Alnwick to Wooler had been agreed in principle with the majority of the owners of the land that it crossed. The figures quoted in support were wildly optimistic. It was estimated that the cost would be as low as £6,000 per mile including '...the formation of the tunnel, and from minute calculations made by experienced and practical men from the most accurate data, a large percentage will accrue from the capital invested.' [21]

The NER was also interested in 1859 [22], and later proposed incorporating the line into a larger scheme. The *Alnwick Mercury* reported on 15 April 1861:-

> 'The North-Eastern Railway Company have taken into serious consideration the advantages not only of forming a line from Alnwick to Wooler, but of continuing it to Edinburgh, and making it a main line, by which *fifteen miles* will be saved on this principal route to the Scottish capital....'

> 'The Duke of Northumberland, Lord Ravensworth, and other land-owners are favourable to the scheme, and ready to contribute towards the expenses. The railway company's engineer is at present engaged on the inspection of the proposed route by way of Glanton, Wooler and Cornhill to Edinburgh; and until his report is made it would be difficult to say much on the practicability of the scheme.'

As already mentioned, the NER was encountering extreme opposition from the NBR to its Bill for the merger with the Newcastle & Carlisle, and the timing of this threat of a rival main line to Edinburgh, however impractical, may have just been a ploy to unsettle the NBR. By 15 March 1862 the same newspaper reported that the NER had not replied to a letter asking what its intentions were, and concluded: '...it would appear that the North-Eastern Company were rather inclined to back out, and had a wish to shelve the line.' The NBR withdrew its opposition to the Amalgamation Bill in 1862, and it was granted the royal assent on 17 July. The NER then lost interest in this part of Northumberland for nearly two decades.

When the NCR proposal of forming a line from Rothbury to Wooler looked like becoming a reality, in 1862, it caused some consternation to the people of Alnwick, who obviously regarded trade with the area along the east of the Cheviots up to Wooler as their prerogative. They were concerned that this would disappear if the town was bypassed by the proposed railway. More surprisingly, the people of Wooler and Cornhill also were not happy with the NCR proposal, even though it would have served them both. Public meetings were held in the district and the NER directors received at least three petitions, during 1862, for a railway either between Alnwick and Kelso via Wooler or just from Alnwick to Wooler. The signatories included Lords Durham, Grey, Tankerville and Lady Waterford together with many of the landowners and tradespeople of the districts.[23] The petitioners pledged to give every assistance and to take shares in the company if the NER would undertake to build the railway.

By 1862 many hard lessons had been learnt in railway investment so their reason for wanting the NER scheme is not hard to find. The promoters of a private railway would have to find almost all of the money locally, and there was no chance of any return on their capital. Investment in a scheme supported by the NBR would mean that less local money was needed at less risk. However, the dividends on NBR shares had dropped from a norm of around 3% to 1% by the end of 1862. On the other hand the NER, with the second largest receipts in Britain, was paying around 4½% dividend - so a condition of investment in that company would be no hardship.[24] Sir Horace St. Paul, later to be a NCR director, remarked 'we are in the position of courters [sic], and are courting the North-Eastern at present as being the most desirable "bargain"' [25]. The NER was already fully committed on major projects so the plea fell on deaf ears. It seemed content just to watch the progress, and, as the NCR was undersubscribed, things did not go well for it. It is worth dwelling briefly on the fortunes of this scheme as it shows the problems of building an independently promoted railway in Central Northumberland.

On 28 July 1863 Parliament authorised the NCR to raise £270,000 in shares and £90,000 in loans to construct a line from a junction with the NBR at Scots' Gap to Cornhill, a total distance of 49¾ miles. Richard Hodgson's dubious policies were finally renounced in 1866 and he was deposed as the NBR's chairman; consequently that railway's interest in the NCR diminished. On 12 April 1867 an Act was obtained permitting the abandonment of the northern part of the scheme. This reduced it to a mere 13 miles from Scots' Gap to Rothbury; the authorised capital became £75,000 in shares with a £25,000 loan. Even before the next half-yearly meeting the chairman, Earl Grey, and the directors were recommending that the company be wound up and the half-completed works abandoned as no further capital was forthcoming. Many would-be subscribers had failed to pay the calls on their shares, and some large landowners had given no support whatsoever.[26] The line was saved by a hairsbreadth by the Railway Companies Act of 1867, which had become law less than a fortnight before the half-yearly meeting at the end of August. This Act allowed companies in difficulties to issue shares at a discount in certain conditions. Having agreed in principle to invoke the new Act, a special meeting was called to authorise further capital to be raised on a discount basis. The old Duke of Northumberland had died just prior to the critical August meeting. He had been very supportive of the line so it was fortunate that his successor was of a similar mind as it was the new Duke's investment that enabled work to restart and the line to be completed.[25]

In the final phase new personalities took over. Earl Grey was replaced as chairman by Sir Walter Trevelyan, and the engineer for the line, J. F. Tone, resigned and was replaced by Mr. (later Sir) George Barclay Bruce. By 31 December 1867 £42,779 had been spent, and Tone estimated the cost of finishing the line would be another £40,000.[27] The additional cost actually came to £54,383, and led to a bitter argument between Hodgson and Bruce.[28] The line was opened on 1 November 1870 and, somewhat in debt, it was taken over at a bargain price by the NBR (Act 18 July 1872), who, after a five year break, had just started to pay a dividend again. They had to pay only £9,600 to discharge the NCR's liabilities, and it was agreed that the mortgage dept of £21,706 was to be converted to NBR 4% debenture stock from 1877.[29] The line, which carried 100 passengers a day, became the last of the NBR's collection of unremunerative branch lines in Northumberland.

The NBR had achieved little or nothing from these railways, and those who had gained the most were the people of rural Northumberland who, for the first time in history, had benefited from a Scottish invasion!

## ENDNOTES

1. W. W. Tomlinson, *North Eastern Railway: Its Rise and Development* (1914 reprinted 1967) p. 32. The first Act for a railway in this area was granted in 1811 for a line from Kelso to Spittal (Tweedmouth). It was not built, but did include the first mention in an Act allowing for the carriage of passengers by rail.
2. W. W. Tomlinson (2), *Comprehensive Guide to Northumberland* (1887 and numerous reprints) p. 372.
3. Ibid. p. 474.
4. *Report of the Officers of the Railway Department to the President of the Board of Trade 1841,* (Smith-Barlow Report) pp.28-9, 78 and Appendix 13. The Report concluded: 'The cuttings, embankments and tunnels are of a formidable description, so much indeed, that if no other line were attainable, we should be reluctant to recommend this project.' M. E. Bowman, who proposed the direct line from Newcastle to Longhoughton via Morpeth, refers to the Newcastle to Dalkeith as 'Mr. Rennie's line' in his evidence. However, all the official references give Mr. Remington the credit for this impossible route.
5. D/NCP/4/29 Deposited Plan Tyne & Wear Archives.
6. Addyman & Haworth, *Robert Stephenson: Railway Engineer* (2005) pp. 89, 91.
7. Tomlinson, p. 522, also ZAN M16/B7 Northumberland County Archives.
8. ZAN M16/B7 gives prospectuses for some of these schemes. The figures are wildly optimistic e.g. Morpeth to Rothbury £80,000 (the 13 miles from Scots' Gap to Rothbury cost over £90,000 to build) and Central Northumberland £260,000.
9. *Proc. I. C. E. Vol. 26,* pp. 73-4.
10. Also known as Richard Hodgson Huntley.
11. J. Baxter Langley MRCS, former editor of the *Newcastle Daily Chronicle,* pamphlet on *The Dangers of the North British Railway Policy* published in two editions in 1861. Private collection.
12. John Thomas, *The North British Railway Vol. 1* (1969) pp. 82-4. Also PRO RAIL 527/1798.
13. PRO RAIL 527/1800, NER's petition against this amalgamation.
14. *Proc. I. C. E. Vol.67* pp. 399-402. Obituaries.
15. Langley, op. cit.
16. PRO RAIL 527/1805.
17. Thomas, op. cit. p.104.
18. Tomlinson, p. 588-595. It cost the NER £37,000 in legal expenses to defeat this Bill.
19. *Report of the Alnwick Railway Committee* Jan. 1845, North of England Institute of Mining and Mechanical Engineers, Tract No.246.
20. *Alnwick Journal,* 17 Dec. 1859.
21. Ibid. 15 May 1860.
22. *The Engineer Vol. 8,* 23 December 1859 reported: 'Arrangements are being made to establish a line between Alnwick and Wooler. The Duke of Northumberland has approved and the NER is considering it in view of the Cambo [Scots' Gap] to Wooler proposal, and the need to defend its own interests and to connect the north-western part of the county with its own lines.'
23. PRO RAIL 527/1677 and 1724.
24. *Bradshaw's Railway Manual, Shareholders' Guide and Directory*, various editions.
25. *Alnwick Mercury,* 6 July 1887
26. Ibid. 15 March 1862.
27. *Bradshaw*, 1869 edition p. 265.
28. The working drawings (private collection) show modifications to Tone's gradients to reduce the earthworks particularly in the region of Font Burn (NZ 052938) and Forest Burn (NZ 060961). However, in some cases the excavation had to be increased as his proposed cutting slopes were found to be too steep for a safe angle of repose in the excavated material.
29. *Bradshaw*, 1869 to 1888 editions. S. C. Jenkins, *The Rothbury Branch* (1991) says, incorrectly, that the total cost was £54,000 giving the ludicrously low figure of just over £4,000 per mile.

## CHAPTER TWO: AUTHORISATION

Local interest in further railway facilities in north Northumberland had remained active through the 1870s but no workable idea had emerged. There was a strong feeling that the area was being stultified by the lack of an efficient transport system. The road network, at that time, was very similar to the present day system of maintained highways, and the transport needs of the area were served by numerous carriers' carts. It may seem strange in our ultra road-oriented era that before the Alnwick & Cornhill was built a local newspaper described the district as: '…having no system of communication except the old system of road conveyance which is quite inadequate for the requirements of the present day.'[1] In the 1870s the situation on the main highways throughout the country was becoming acute as a result of railway competition severely reducing turnpike revenues to a level insufficient for their maintenance. This led to a growing public resistance to paying the tolls and to Parliament abolishing the Turnpike Trusts, with the responsibility for raising maintenance funds transferred to the parishes, Boards of Health, etc. Obviously, the inhabitants of a district without a railway were unfairly disadvantaged, both by the high cost of road transport, and the greater usage of their roads leading to higher maintenance costs. There was probably a lot of truth in one of the contemporary arguments in favour of a railway – that its appearance would enhance the profitability of an average farm by about £200 per annum.

All the towns and villages served by the NER enjoyed a minimum weekday service of three passenger trains in each direction and, generally, a pick-up goods. Wooler, by the 1880s the only market town in the North East without a railway, had, by contrast, a daily mail coach to and from Alnwick, which carried four people and took two-and-a-half hours for the single journey.[2] The other public service was a return trip to Belford, in summer, to connect with the mid-day main-line trains to the north and the south.[3] Goods traffic cost at least five times as much by horse drawn conveyance as it did by train, and, for example, a return trip from Wooler to Belford (21 miles) could take the best part of a day. Moving livestock on foot was even more time-consuming.

The Light Railway Act, making it easier to promote and build local railways, did not come into force until 1896, but the Regulation of Railways Act 1868 and the Tramways Act 1870 allowed some low-cost rural railways to be projected, and a few to be built. The North Northumberland Agricultural Railway anticipated the provisions of the later Act. This scheme, to provide a line from Rothbury to Cornhill with a branch from Glanton to Alnwick, was promoted at local meetings in the autumn of 1880. The engineer for the project, George Lambton of Newcastle, stated that it was not to be a tramway but the line would follow the existing highways wherever possible 'to save the cost of fencing.' There would be no stations but trains would stop anywhere to pick up or set down passengers, and sidings would be provided at every farm. Passenger fares were quoted at one penny per mile and goods rates at about one-and-a-half pence per ton mile. His estimate for the construction of about £2,500 per mile was optimistic, as the cost of the permanent way material alone for a light railway would be over £1,000 per mile.[4]

Although the proposal was given a mixed reception in Alnwick it was enthusiastically received in meetings held elsewhere, but it failed the ultimate test of being able to raise capital. However, it did concentrate local minds again on the fact that if they were to have a railway at all it would have to be at someone else's expense. The people of Alnwick, with their favoured route connecting two NER branches, hoped that this rich company might be persuaded, at this stage, to build a proper railway. If the line turned out to be unprofitable any investment that they had to make for it would be rewarded with the dividend paid on the whole NER system.

In one way there could not have been a better time to approach the NER as, after a four year recession, the company's financial position, at the end of 1880, must have seemed extremely rosy to the directors and shareholders. The gross revenue had increased to £6.4 million - 15.5% over the previous year. The working expenses expressed as a percentage of this gross revenue were still under 50% and, in fact, were lower than when the company was formed in 1854. This was to result in the dividend on ordinary shares for 1880 being declared at 8¼ per cent. The one thing that would be unfavourable to new railway construction was the increasing difficulty in raising capital. Due to the recession in the late 1870s the board had had to put a severe brake on capital spending. During the 20 years prior to 1878 capital expenditure had exceeded an average of £1.6 million per annum, but its purpose was mainly to provide lines and facilities necessary to handle the burgeoning traffic. In the 1880s capital expenditure was to be restrained to an average of £425,000 per annum. The Alnwick & Cornhill would use one-tenth of the decade's capital allocation.[5]

In the big spending years of the early 1870s the agricultural districts of, what is now known as, North Yorkshire had been particularly favoured. The market towns of Hawes, Helmsley, Masham and Kirkbymoorside had all been served by railways authorised between 1866 and 1871. The year 1880 saw the bankrupt, independently promoted coast line from Loftus to Whitby being completed by the NER and its own Pickering to Seamer branch under construction. The latter ran most of its length within three to four miles of its York to Scarborough branch of 1845.[6] Some of these lines had little better traffic potential than the district between Alnwick and Wooler, but, in contrast with North Yorkshire, there had been virtually no branch line investment by the NER in Northumberland for 30 years.

The reason for this disparity is not hard to find. In 1872, when the NER representatives were giving evidence to justify their monopoly in the North East to the Joint Select Committee on Railway Companies' Amalgamations, they had said that the public could rely on the director in their locality to be aware of local pressures. But what if they did not have a local director? There were roughly four times as many NER shareholders in Yorkshire as there were in Northumberland and as a result the chairman, deputy chairman and nine of the 18 directors lived in Yorkshire. There were only two directors in Northumberland; both resided in the Tyne Valley about 50 miles from the Wooler district. This pattern was to change, but without a local director it was obviously up to the local bodies and landowners interested in a railway to put their case. The railway committee had been resurrected in Alnwick, and they had gone as far as to re-evaluate possible routes for a line, particularly in the immediate vicinity of the town. The Alnwick newspaper printed the monthly traffic figures for the NER system, so those interested could not fail to see the company's happy financial position in 1880, although they would probably be unaware of the capital restraints.

With the impetus of the recent discussions about the North Northumberland Agricultural Railway, the Alnwick and Canongate Board of Health (the predecessors of the Rural District Council) and some local landowners decided to make their own approach to the NER. After sounding out T. E. Harrison's opinion, they formally arranged to meet the new NER chairman, John Dent Dent, and some directors in Newcastle to ask them to re-open the case for a railway between Alnwick and the Kelso branch. They must have been fairly happy when they were not rebuffed, and were told that the NER would look favourably on the scheme if the landowners would be prepared to sell the necessary land at fair agricultural prices and assist in other ways.[7]

News of their success sparked off a minor railway mania in the district in the New Year, leading to a series of meetings being held from Newcastle to the Border. These were in favour either of the Alnwick and Cornhill or more extensive railway facilities. In January and February 1881 meetings were held in Rothbury, Wooler, Newcastle and Kelso as well as in some of the villages. On Thursday 3 February when landowners and gentry met in the White Swan at Alnwick to discuss the land prices, as requested by the NER, resolutions were passed not only in favour of the original scheme, but also a counter-proposal for a line from the Tyne to the Tweed through Central Northumberland. However, the landowners represented at the meeting decided to make the necessary land available for *a* railway scheme, and a deputation was elected to make an early approach to the NER directors with their answer.[8]

A meeting held in Rothbury on 31 January led to a further meeting in Newcastle on 12 February, chaired by Sir Charles Trevelyan, when it was resolved that: -

> '...further railway accommodation for central Northumberland and the adjoining parts of Roxburghshire was much required, and that nothing short of a line through the centre of Northumberland from Newcastle to the neighbourhood of

Kelso, giving facilities to Rothbury, Alnwick, Wooler and the Bowmont and Kale valleys, will supply this accommodation.' [9]

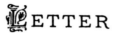

# Central Northumberland Railway.

## LETTER

### TO THE

## DIRECTORS

### OF THE

## NORTH EASTERN RAILWAY.

### A Short Statement of Facts,

#### BY

## JAMES BALFOUR KERR,

#### BANKER.

*"It should suffice each of us to know that if we have laboured with purity of purpose in any good cause we MUST have contributed to its success; that the degree in which we have contributed is a matter of infinitely small concern; and, still more, that the consciousness of having so contributed, however obscurely and unnoticed, should be our sufficient if our sole reward. Let us cherish this faith: it is a duty.*

W. R. GREG.

### KELSO:
#### CRAIG & THOMSON, *CHRONICLE* OFFICE.
#### 1881.

**Fig. 2.1: J. B. Kerr's pamphlet of 1881 outlining Kelso's views on the railway proposals.**

It added that the foregoing should be put into effect 'either by negotiations with existing companies or by an independent company.' This proposal was to emerge as the Central Northumberland Railway (CNR), and its supporters, which now included the Mayor of Newcastle, fondly hoped that the tradespeople of Newcastle and Gateshead would help to raise the one million pounds capital required for this impractical single line railway. Unfortunately for their scheme, unlike Hull, there was no dissatisfaction on Tyneside with the services provided by the NER. (It was the major problems of co-ordinating railway and dock expansion in Hull that enabled the Hull and Barnsley Railway to break the NER's monopoly at this time.)

The Kelso meetings of 18 and 21 February passed similar resolutions to Newcastle's but added their own grievance about the distance of Kelso station from the town, and the possibility of a new spur into it from the NBR.[10] Another Kelso proposal, which did not gain other support, was to continue the line northwards to join the Waverley route near Fountain Hall station.[11]

As a result of these meetings the weight of opinion was very much in favour of the larger CNR scheme. Not surprisingly, when the deputation from the Alnwick meeting saw the directors of the NER, on 24 March 1881, they found that they were outranked and outnumbered by the supporters of the CNR led by Sir Charles Trevelyan. The NER chairman said bluntly that he could not impose on his shareholders such a large expense as the CNR unless the landowners, who would derive the greatest benefit, would not only make their land available cheaply but help with the capital. Councillor Adam Robertson (1834-1894), for the Alnwick contingent, said that he had brought a favourable answer regarding the land prices, and he hoped that the chairman's remarks did not apply to the less ambitious original scheme. What the chairman did not say, but the Alnwick party already knew, was that the NER had begun a survey for the Alnwick and Cornhill at the beginning of February.[12] However, the NER was still prepared to give the CNR supporters a fair chance if they could prove their ability to raise substantial capital support, even though there was the in-built problem of running powers over the NBR Rothbury branch.

A committee of leading CNR supporters had been elected, and they met in Newcastle on 23 April 1881 to consider a letter from the NER requesting them to appoint a deputation to meet the directors with an answer on the capital support and land prices.[13] By August it was obvious that the CNR could not fulfil the NER's conditions, but they still could not accept that the abandonment of their scheme was inevitable. A reminder of the problems with the Northumberland Central Railway, fourteen years earlier, should have led them to the obvious sensible decision.

The Marquis of Tweeddale (later to be NBR chairman), who was in favour of the CNR, was more of a realist and stated that there was no probability of the railway being made if the cost exceeded the very low figure of £5,000 per mile. Using T. E. Harrison's yardstick, quoted in chapter 1, this would be based on a revenue of £10 per mile per week, which was the very best that the adjacent area could be expected to raise. Cornelius and George Lundie, who hailed from Kelso and were both civil engineers, proposed a narrow gauge railway in the spring of 1881. This was the only way to get the construction costs down to an acceptable figure. Cornelius Lundie had considerable railway experience, originally as the manager of the Blyth & Tyne and currently as general manager and engineer of the Rhymney Railway. Significantly, he and his brother proposed a three feet gauge railway only from Rothbury to Kelso, utilising mixed gauge track over the NBR at the start and finish. They estimated that the scheme would cost under £250,000 for the 47¼ miles, and that it would generate traffic worth £24,525 per annum, i.e. £10 per mile per week. Although, they detailed their arguments in a pamphlet published on 1 July 1881, their proposal was not entertained by the CNR committee.[14]

A meeting was held at Wallington Hall (the home of the Trevelyan family) on 10 August 1881 to set up a guarantee fund to defray the preliminary expenses of the survey and parliamentary work for an independent CNR Bill. £5,000 was required but over £8,000 was enthusiastically pledged. William Shelford, engineer of the Hull & Barnsley Railway, was asked to prepare the scheme, but 'the expense of the survey was not to exceed £1,000'[15].

After receiving a signed, but undated, agreement from the owners of over half the land necessary for the A&C, the NER board decided, on 21 October 1881, to proceed with that railway. In accordance with Parliamentary Standing Orders, notice was given on 1 November 1881 that the NER would be applying for the necessary powers in the next session of Parliament (fig. 2.2).

In March 1882 both the CNR and NER (Alnwick & Cornhill Railway) Bills were considered by a Select Committee of the House of Commons. Mr. Hardcastle M. P. chaired the Committee, and the other members were Mr. Colman, Colonel Kennard and Baron de Worms. As far back as 1853 the Railway and Canal Bills Committee had recommended to

Parliament that a board of *experts* should be set up to review proposals for new railways in preference to the normal system of 'volunteering' M. Ps to Select Committees regardless of any knowledge they may have of railways or the district to be served. In this case north-country Members; Earl Percy, Sir Matthew Ridley, J. W. Pease and Mr. Albert Grey were in attendance to give assistance.

IN PARLIAMENT.

SESSION 1882.

# NORTH-EASTERN RAILWAY.
## (ALNWICK AND CORNHILL BRANCH.)

Construction of New Railway between Alnwick and Cornhill. Additional Capital. Amendment of Acts.

NOTICE IS HEREBY GIVEN that application is intended to be made to Parliament in the next Session by the North-Eastern Railway Company (hereinafter called the Company) for an Act for the following purposes, or some of them, (that is to say):—

To authorise the Company to make and maintain the Railway hereinafter described, with all proper Stations, Sidings, Approaches, Works and conveniences connected therewith, (that is to say);—

A Railway commencing in the Township of Alnwick and Parish of Alnwick in the County of Northumberland by a Junction with the Company's Alnwick Branch, at a point thereon about 150 yards (measured along that Branch in a South-Easterly direction) from the Platform Entrance to the Passengers Booking-Office at the Alnwick Station thereon, and terminating in the Township of Cornhill and Parish of Norham in the said County of Northumberland by a Junction with the Company's Kelso Branch, at or near the Bridge carrying that Branch over the public road at the Coldstream Station thereon; which intended Railway will pass from, in, through, or into, or be situate within the several Parishes, Townships, and extra-parochial or other places following, or some of them, (that is to say) Alnwick, Alnwick Southside, Edlingham, Bolton, Broom Park, Learchild, Lemmington, Abberwick, Whittingham, Glanton, Shawdon and Woodhouse, Barton, Thrunton, Eglingham, West Lilburn, East Lilburn, New Bewick, Wooperton, Beanley, Brandon, Hedgeley, Crawley, Branton, Ilderton, Middleton Hall, North Middleton, South Middleton, Roseden, Chatton, Coldmartin, Doddington, Earle, Wooler, Humbleton Kirknewton, Paston, Kilham, Howtel, Crookhouse, Lanton, Westnewton, Yeavering, Coupland, Akeld, Carham, Moneylaws, Learmouth, Downham, Mindrum, Ford, Crookham, Norham and Cornhill, all in the said County of Northumberland.

To authorise the Company to purchase and take by compulsion or agreement and to hold lands houses and buildings, or any estates or interests in or easements over lands: houses and buildings, situate in all or some of the before mentioned Parishes, Townships, and extra-parochial and other places for the purposes of the proposed Railway and Works, including a portion of certain common or commonable Land in the said Township of Alnwick and Parish of Alnwick, called or known by the name of the Forest of Aydon otherwise Haydon or Alnwick Moor, of which it is estimated that fifteen acres or thereabouts are intended to be taken by the Company, and to make provision as to the sale to the Company by the owners of or others interested in the said common or commonable land of the portion so required.

To empower the Company to purchase so much of any property as they may require for the purposes of the intended Act without being subject to the liability imposed by Section 92 of "The Lands Clauses Consolidation Act, 1845."

To alter, vary, or extinguish all existing rights, privileges and exemptions connected with any lands, houses, and buildings proposed to be purchased, taken, used or interfered with under the powers, or for the purposes of the intended Act, or which would in any manner impede or interfere with the objects or purposes of the intended Act, or any of them, and to confer, vary, alter, or extinguish other rights privileges and exemptions.

To authorise the crossing, diverting, altering, or stopping up, whether temporarily or permanently, of all turnpike roads, highways and other roads, footpaths, rivers, streams, canals, navigations, tramways, bridges, and other works within or adjoining to the before-mentioned parishes, townships, extra-parochial and other places which it may be necessary or convenient to cross, divert, alter, or stop up, or interfere with for the purposes of the intended Act, or any of them, and to appropriate the sites thereof respectively to the use of the Company and purposes of their undertaking.

To empower the Company to demand, take and recover tolls, rates, and charges for or in respect of the use of the proposed Railway and works, and to alter existing tolls, rates and charges, and to confer, vary, or extinguish exemptions from the payment of tolls, rates, and charges.

To empower the Company to increase their Capital, and to raise further sums of money for all or any of the purposes of the intended Act, and for the general purposes of the Company, by the creation and issue of new shares or Stock, with or without a guaranteed or preference dividend or other rights or privileges attached thereto, and by the creation and issue of Debenture Stock, and by borrowing, or by any of such means, and also to apply to all or any of such purposes any capital or funds belonging to the Company.

AND NOTICE IS HEREBY FURTHER GIVEN that on or before the 30th day of November instant, maps, plans, and sections relating to the objects of the intended Act. with a book of reference to such plans, and a copy of this Notice, as published in the London *Gazette*, will be deposited for public inspection with the Clerk of the Peace for the County of Northumberland, at his Office at Newcastle-upon-Tyne, and that on or before the said 30th day of November instant a Copy of so much of the said plans, sections, and Book of reference as relates to each Parish in or through which the proposed Railway and Works are intended to be made, and also a Copy of this Notice as published in the London *Gazette*, will be deposited with the Parish Clerk of each such parish, at his place of abode, and as regards any extra-parochial place with the Clerk of some adjoining parish, at his place of abode.

And it is proposed by the intended Act, if need be, to alter, amend, extend and enlarge, or to repeal all or some of the powers and provisions of the several local and personal Acts of Parliament following, or some of them, that is to say—17 and 18 Vic., cap. 211 ; 26 and 27 Vic., cap. 122 ; 28 Vic., cap. 111 ; 33 Vic., cap. 7 ; and 37 and 38 Vic., cap. 105 ; respectively relating to the Company and its undertaking; and the several Acts in the before-mentioned Acts respectively, or any of them, recited or referred to, and any other Acts of Parliament which it may be necessary to alter, amend, or repeal, for the purposes to be authorised by the intended Act, and to make other provision in lieu of the provisions so altered, amended, or repealed.

On or before the 21st day of December next Printed Copies of the intended Act or Bill will be deposited in the Private Bill Office of the House of Commons.

Dated this 15th day of November, 1881.

RICHARDSON, GUTCH, & CO.,

Solicitors, York.

SHERWOOD & CO.,

7, Great George-street, Westminster,
Parliamentary Agents.

**Figure 2.2: the Parliamentary notice for the NER 1882 Bill giving details of the route to be followed and the powers required.**

18

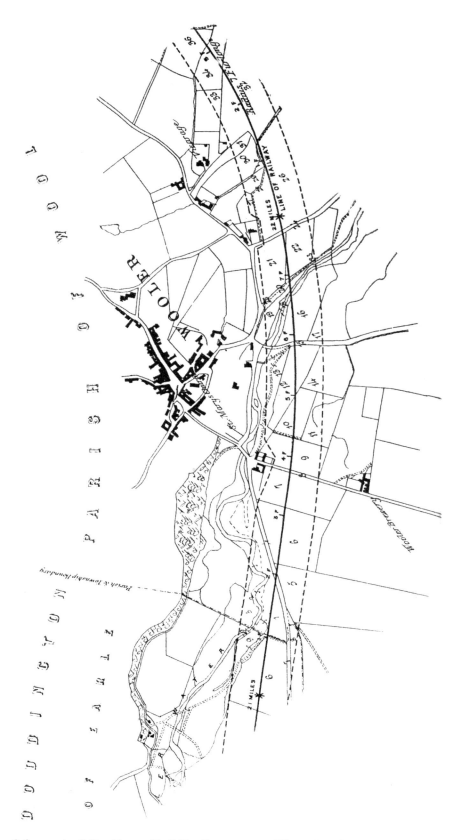

**Figure 2.3: part of the Deposited Parliamentary Plan showing the proposal for Wooler. The limits of deviation of 110 yards are shown by the dotted lines on each side of the railway centre line.**

Mr. Rodwell Q.C. appeared for the NER and was accompanied by Mr. Bidder Q.C.; Mr. Pope Q.C. represented the Central Northumberland. The main witnesses for the NER were: John Dent Dent (chairman), Henry Tennant (general manager) and T. E. Harrison (engineer). Sir Charles Trevelyan and William Shelford C.E. gave the crucial evidence for the CNR. Newcastle Council was represented by its Mayor, Town Clerk and engineer. Mr. Milvain represented the property owners opposed to the Alnwick and Cornhill.[16]

Mr. Rodwell opened for the NER by contrasting the schemes: -

'...it [the CNR] would require, in round numbers, £1,000,000, whereas the capital required for the North Eastern scheme was £375,000. The North Eastern line would be 35 miles long, that of the Central Northumberland 75 miles. The latter would go through a district without any population, without any minerals, yet sanction was asked to the expenditure of an enormous sum for the purpose of such a wild speculation as this. It would be unjustifiable for the North Eastern to run into such a wild and extravagant expenditure without a prospect of any return. Here, for £400,000, they had a scheme that had received the sanction of more than half the landowners on the line. Not only that, but such landowners as his Grace the Duke of Northumberland, Lord Tankerville, Lord Ravensworth, and others had given their land for the construction of the line at 25 years' agricultural [rent] value, to include severance. The landowners opposed were Lord Grey, Mr. Lambton, and others who were simply persons who preferred the Central Northumberland scheme.'

The NER chairman, John Dent Dent, started by recounting the history of its proposal back to the Alnwick Local Board's deputation in the autumn of 1880. He then discussed the disadvantages of the CNR only being able to have a terminus to the north of Newcastle, without connections to the lines to the south (the NER would have been able to bring a line into its system at Gosforth or Scotswood). He had been over the district between Rothbury and Whittingham and did not feel able to support a line through it. (An unproductive seven-mile detour to the west, via Alnham, would have been needed to avoid a tunnel three to four miles long immediately north of Rothbury.) He added that both lines were practically identical from Whittingham to Mindrum.

Mr. (later Sir) Jacob Wilson, Lord Tankerville's estate manager and member of the Royal Commission on Agriculture, gave the best description of the district and its prospects. He considered it was: -

'...principally agricultural, three-fifths of it being arable and two-fifths pasture. The line would develop the district in conveying produce in the shape of corn, beef, mutton, and wool, and sundry other articles from farmers, at the same conveying lime and artificial manures, coal, and other necessaries to the farms.' He thought 'the North Eastern scheme by far the best', but would prefer it to be extended from Mindrum to Yetholm and Kelso. 'He looked to a great future for Wooler. It would be an important centre for auction marts of all kinds of agricultural produce, both cattle and sheep and corn, which would come not only from the district, but from the big merchants from Coldstream, Berwick, and also Newcastle and Sunderland. It had already a woollen manufactory, a corn mill, and brewery. ...If he were sending goods he would send them by Alnwick, for nine-tenths of the produce of the district went to places south of Newcastle – to Manchester and other places.'

T. E. Harrison defended the choice of Cornhill as the northern terminus by a rather dubious argument: -

'It was suggested that the North Eastern line, by going to Cornhill, instead of Kelso, pointed the wrong way. Now, the only bridge across the Tweed was between Cornhill and Coldstream. The whole of Berwickshire lay to that side of the river, which was a very fine extent of country, and the only point by which they could really get to it was by Cornhill. If they did not go to Cornhill they practically excluded the whole of that portion of the country from any benefits which would result from the formation of the line.'

The NER Kelso branch already served Berwickshire via the Coldstream Bridge. Many other witnesses generally in favour of the NER scheme were examined and the case for the CNR was then heard.

The Dukes of Northumberland and Roxburghe, the Earl of Ravensworth, Newcastle Corporation, the Committee of Stewards, Wardens and Freemen of Newcastle, the NER, NBR and Marchburn, Kelso and Lauder Road Trustees all had petitioned against the CNR. Both Newcastle Corporation and the Freemen were petitioning against the CNR's intended interference with the Town Moor.[16] The NBR's petition against the CNR was, for reasons unknown, withdrawn after the first day of the hearing.

Sir Charles Trevelyan started his evidence for the CNR by attacking the NER. He felt the Company 'had sucked the marrow of their county without giving them the railway accommodation they wanted.' He went on: 'Mr. Dent and others have taunted us with not accepting the offer of the North-Eastern Company, which was to raise and pay over to them £250,000 under circumstances which would have caused a loss of 20 per cent of the capital.' His real objection was not to the 20 per cent but 'that it was impossible to combine an unorganised and miscellaneous body of country gentlemen ...to attempt to make a railway ourselves.' Regardless of this, and having failed with the NER, 'we directed our attention in fulfilment of our trust to the formation of a substantial and independent Company.' They had paid the preliminary expenses and deposited £45,000 in compliance with Parliamentary standing orders, but had, as yet, made no attempt to issue a prospectus to raise money for the line's construction. The arguments ranged over many options but the crucial point was raised in the Committee chairman's last remark: 'We have asked for financial evidence, and we have not had any very satisfactory financial evidence as yet – that is, **you have not given us any idea how you are going to raise the money for this concern**.'

After the evidence was complete the Committee took only half-an-hour to formulate its decision. It found in favour of the NER scheme but only of the southern part of the CNR i.e. from Newcastle to the NBR at Scots' Gap. As politicians, in their attempt 'to be all things to all men' they expressed the hope that the NER would assist with the Newcastle to Scots' Gap and connect it with its own system at Newcastle. They also felt that the NER should provide a link from Rothbury to the A&C. On the final day of the hearing the committee sorted out various clauses in the Bills that had been proved, particularly with regard to the level crossings on the routes.[17]

The idea of building the part of the CNR line from Scots' Gap to Newcastle shows little appreciation of the situation as the direct line would have generated very little traffic. An Act for the South Northumberland Railway had been granted in 1865, with Robert Hodgson as one of the five directors. It was to run from a proposed Blyth & Tyne terminus near Walbottle (Act 1861), west of Newcastle, via Stamfordham to Scots' Gap. Neither scheme got beyond authorisation as, by that time, there was a rail service from Scots' Gap to Newcastle via Morpeth, and one via Reedsmouth to Hexham. Later, when the NER built its short Ponteland branch along the more populated southern end of the B&T route, in anticipation of housing developments that did not materialise, it was only open to passengers from 1905 until 1929. The only evidence that the NER may have given a passing thought to providing the central link from Whittingham to Rothbury is an undated sketch in one of T. E. Harrison's notebooks. This shows two branches diverging from the south end of the island platform at Whittingham station (fig.2.4).

*The Newcastle Daily Journal* for 23 March 1882 summed up the situation perfectly: -

'The decision of the Select Committee on the Northumbrian Railways Bills accords pretty well with the general expectation. It likewise shows a sincere and laudable desire on the part of the Committee to promote as far as they possibly could the substantial interests of the district. It is, of course, not always within the powers of a Parliamentary Committee to effect that object, for it can only sanction and recommend, and in a case in which the power and the will to execute lies with capitalists and public corporations, there is often a long interval between such sanction and recommendation and the performance. It would not have been reasonable for the committee to reject the Bill of the North Eastern Railway

Company, which contained a distinct and certain offer to make a railway from Alnwick to Wooler and Cornhill, in order to prefer a more ambitious scheme, which was merely laid before Parliament by a group of country gentlemen, who could give no security whatever that the capital would ever be provided to make their line. Even the most enthusiastic supporters of the Central Northumberland line were unable to deny that the branch offered by the North-Eastern will be of local value as far as it goes. To the residents in the Alnwick and Wooler districts it offers nearly all they can desire, and there is little wonder that they should be induced to support it, rather than wait on the uncertain chance of a longer line being made by an independent company. Again, the absence of any connection with Alnwick in the Central Northumberland scheme undoubtedly left it open to great objection; for not only did it open up no facilities of communication between that town and district and the Wooler Valley, but it also shut out the population of Central Northumberland from any direct access to the coast between Morpeth and Berwick.'

The NER (Alnwick & Cornhill Railway) Bill got the royal assent on 19 May 1882 with authority to raise £375,000 in shares and £125,000 in loans. The CNR, without any chance of support from the NER, was formally wound up on 10 February 1883 when the liquidation account came to £552. The main supporter, Sir Charles Trevelyan, one time Secretary to the Treasury and Governor of Madras, died in 1886.

## ENDNOTES

1.  *Alnwick Gazette*, 31 May 1884. Road maintenance became the responsibility of the County from 1888.
2.  The mail contract was awarded to William Dunn in October 1861, and given to the NER in 1888.
3.  NER Timetable, 1 July until 30 September 1886.
4.  Alnwick Mercury, 25 Sept. 2 and 9 Oct. 1880.
5.  Tomlinson, pp. 776-8.
6.  Cook and Hoole, *NER Historical Maps*.
7.  *Alnwick Mercury*, 26 March 1881.
8.  Ibid. 12 February 1881.
9.  James Balfour Kerr *Central Northumberland Railway,* a pamphlet addressed to the NER directors 23 March 1881, p. 16.
10. Ibid. p. 7 quotes Sir John Brunlees C. E's letter of 8 April 1880 estimating it would cost £75,000 for a spur into Kelso off the NBR, which needed a bridge over the Tweed.
11. Ibid. p. 5.
12. *Alnwick Mercury,* 12 February and 26 March 1881.
13. Ibid. 30 April 1881.
14. NRO 322/B51.
15. *Alnwick Mercury,* 1 October 1881.
16. *Local Acts Vol. 22* Newcastle Lit. & Phil.
17. *Newcastle Daily Journal.* 15-23 March 1887.

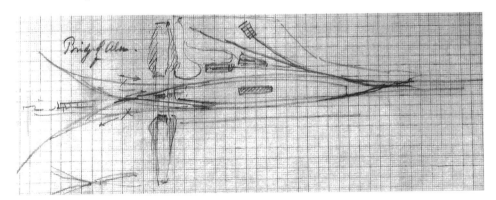

**Figure 2.4: an undated sketch from one of T. E. Harrison's notebooks showing two railways diverging from the south end of Whittingham (Bridge of Aln) station to Alnwick and Rothbury.**

## CHAPTER THREE: THE ROUTE AND ENGINEERING WORKS

The overall control of the planning, design and construction of the Alnwick and Cornhill was in the hands of that remarkable, but now almost forgotten, railwayman, T. E. Harrison. He had started his railway career with Robert Stephenson in the 1830s, first in assisting him in surveying the London & Birmingham Railway and then in building the Stanhope & Tyne Railroad. He had subsequently overseen the construction of two thirds of the NER main line and many other railways. During 1853, in his capacity as general manager and engineer of the York Newcastle & Berwick Railway, he had suggested a merger with two other companies to form the NER. He had been responsible to the NER board for both civil and mechanical engineering functions since its inception in 1854. Also, he had been its first general manager. The engineering of the Alnwick and Cornhill, which was to be his last branch line and the longest projected and built by the NER, posed no problems that had not been encountered already in his long and distinguished career.[1]

Although Alnwick and Cornhill are only 26 miles apart the shortest practical distance for a railway was about 30 miles. This was not achieved because of detours at each end, and the final length came to 35½ miles. The Duke of Northumberland was in support of the railway, but not to such an extent that it could carve though his prime park land at Hulne Park to use the short easy route, north-westwards from Alnwick, up the Aln then via Eglingham (not to be confused with Edlingham) and Lilburn to Wooler. (In 1826 a previous Duke got an Act of Parliament to divert the Eglingham Road [now B 6346] northwards to clear this parkland.) Other factors against this direct route were: it failed to serve the Vale of Whittingham, and the position of Alnwick station, relative to the town, would have made it most difficult, even had the Duke agreed, to circumnavigate the town. Therefore, the NER started the branch in a southerly direction, through the most unproductive land on the line, with a climb of over 400 feet to the summit on Alnwick Moor. T. E. Harrison had been emphatic that it was the correct choice of route when he gave evidence to the Select Committee in 1882.

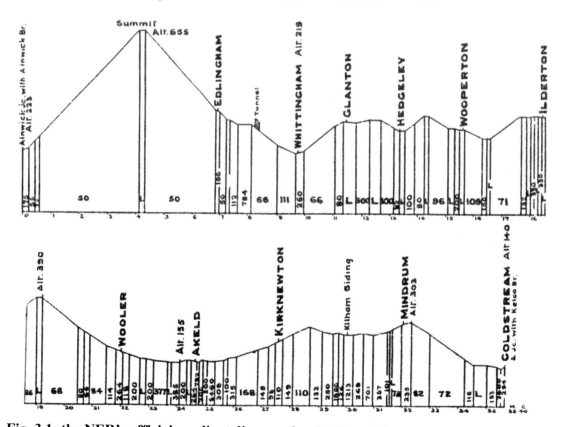

**Fig. 3.1: the NER's official gradient diagram for the line with zero miles at Alnwick.**

The actual route can be followed in detail on the 1:50,000 Ordnance Survey sheets Nos. 74, 75 and 81.[2] For construction purposes the line's mileage was measured from Alnwick to Cornhill, but, as the northern end was the first to open to traffic, the actual mileposts increased in value from north to south. Appendix 1 gives the mileage of all the stations and signal cabins. The line started its enforced climb as soon as it cleared the junction with the Alnmouth branch, and from the half mile point to the summit, just beyond the four mile point, the ruling gradient was 1 in 50. For the final two miles of this climb, from Rugley Wood, the line was mainly in cuttings up to 36 feet deep, through the hard fell sandstone. Further extensive cuttings were needed on the ensuing winding 1 in 50 descent through Lemmington to Edlingham station. Evidence of the difficulties of this length can be seen to this day by the numerous broken rock drills which remain embedded in the cuttings' faces. In all over 500,000 tons of rock were removed from this section. Although Alnwick and Whittingham have the same latitude the line at Edlingham is two miles *south* of them, as it follows a winding course to gain altitude while avoiding long tunnels.

**Plate 3.1: a c.1887 photograph looking towards Alnwick; the Alnwick-Rothbury road is on the right and the deep rock cutting leading to Summit on the skyline. Barter Books**

Immediately beyond Edlingham station the branch swings northwards and the valley of the Edlingham Burn is crossed by a 60 feet high viaduct with five spans of 40 feet. This is the largest structure on the line (plate 3.3). A mile to the north a large cutting, spanned by a three-arched bridge, precedes the sole tunnel on the line. Hillhead Tunnel is a 351 yards long single-track bore at a maximum depth below ground of 125 feet (plate 3.2). The route continues to descend into the fertile Vale of Whittingham with easier gradients through Low Learchild to Whittingham station. A quarter-of-a-mile north of this station the River Aln was crossed by a double-track 58 feet span wrought-iron hog-backed girder bridge. Because of the poor load-bearing of the immediate sub-soil this bridge was supported on 40 feet deep, 5 feet diameter iron cylinders, which still exist.

From Whittingham to Akeld the railway is always within a few hundred feet of the old Morpeth to Coldstream turnpike road (now A 697). The line climbs at 1 in 66 after crossing the Aln for most of the way to Glanton, and fairly extensive earthworks were needed on both sides of Glanton station. Beyond Powburn (Hedgeley station) the River Breamish was crossed with the largest underbridge on the line. Here hog-backed wrought-iron lattice girders 104'-8" long by 10'-2" maximum depth span the 95'-6" watercourse (plate 3.4). The first of the two contracts for building the line ended a little way north of this bridge.

**Plate 3.2: the south entrance to the 351 yard long Hillhead Tunnel. J. F. Mallon.**

**Plate 3.3: Edlingham Viaduct with five spans of 40 feet (one hidden by trees), looking towards Alnwick Moor. The wide pier is a result of foundation problems. J. F. Addyman**

**Plate 3.4: the 95ft 6in span bridge over the River Breamish near Powburn. NERA.**

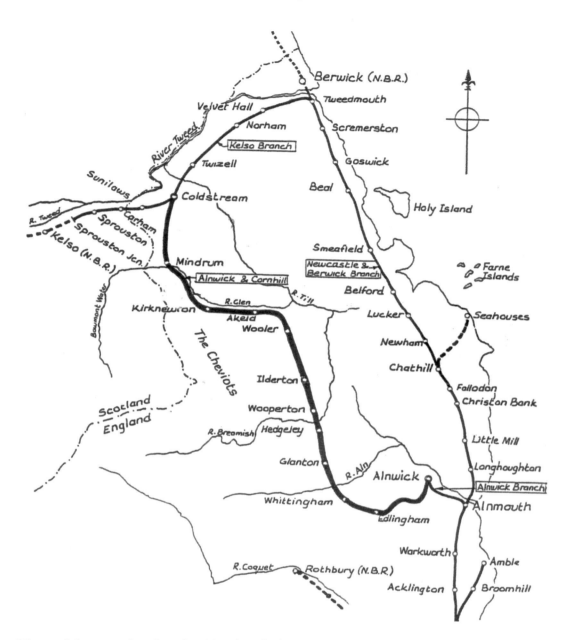

**Figure 3.2: map showing the Alnwick & Cornhill in relation to the other railways of the area. J. F. Addyman**

Compared with its predecessor the early parts of the next contract were easy as the line followed the lie of the land through the irregular glacial deposits with the minimum of earthworks. This resulted in some short steep gradients. At Wooperton the old turnpike road had to be realigned to make room for the railway, to the advantage of future generations of road users. The line kept to the east of the road until it crossed over by a skew bridge immediately south-east of Ilderton station. Three miles further north, just before entering Wooler, the road re-crosses the railway by a large 109 feet skew span plate girder bridge. This 120 year old bridge, with its 8'-6" deep wrought-iron girders still carries the heavy A697 traffic although some propping has been necessary at the quarter span points. The vertical and horizontal alignments of the bridge and its approaches are so good that the majority of today's motorists will not be aware that they are crossing a defunct railway. South of Wooler Station the Wooler Water is crossed by a plate girder bridge with two spans of 34 feet (plate 3.5).

The next three roads in Wooler were crossed on the level even though two were important local roads (now B 6348 and B 6525) to Chatton and Berwick. Railway level crossings have always been a vexed problem, and as early as 1863 the Board of Trade (B.O.T) was given powers to insist on bridges rather than level crossings on new railways; they tried to enforce the rule strictly except on very minor roads. Left to their own devices the railway companies would have provided bridges only where the ground levels dictated, as they were notoriously opposed to many of the sensible B.O.T rules, particularly if they were initially to cost money. At the time that the Alnwick & Cornhill was being built a signalman was paid £1 per week and a gate keeper a lot less. If the box controlling the gates was a block post, as they often were, then the cost of the gates was minimal when compared with a bridge. Although there was no contest with the B.O.T on important highways, when it came to lesser used roads the railways had found ways of getting round the regulations; one of these was used at Wooler.

**Plate 3.5: the two-span wrought-iron plate girder bridge over Wooler Water. NERA.**

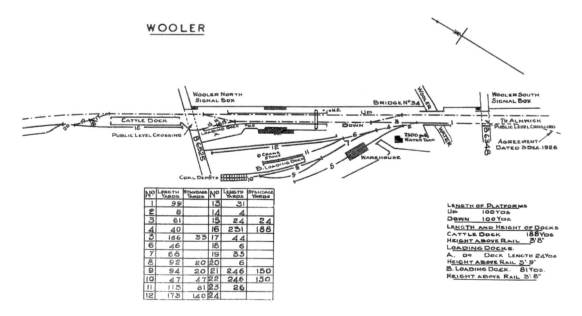

| NO | LENGTH YARDS | STANDAGE YARDS | NO | LENGTH YARDS | STANDAGE YARDS |
|---|---|---|---|---|---|
| 1 | 99 | | 13 | 31 | |
| 2 | 8 | | 14 | 4 | |
| 3 | 61 | | 15 | 24 | 24 |
| 4 | 40 | | 16 | 231 | 188 |
| 5 | 166 | 33 | 17 | 44 | |
| 6 | 46 | | 18 | 6 | |
| 7 | 68 | | 19 | 35 | |
| 8 | 92 | 20 | 20 | 6 | |
| 9 | 94 | 20 | 21 | 246 | 150 |
| 10 | 47 | 47 | 22 | 246 | 150 |
| 11 | 115 | 81 | 23 | 26 | |
| 12 | 173 | 140 | 24 | | |

**Figure 3.3: part of the 1945 siding diagram for Wooler giving the lengths of each track. A new cattle dock was provided at Wooler North in 1900.**

Of the dozen public road level crossings on the Alnwick and Cornhill the two at Wooler certainly justified bridges, but to provide them would have required moving the railway further from the town and diverting the Wooler Water. By February 1882 Richardson, Gutch & Co., the NER's solicitors, had concluded negotiations for the level crossings with the Glendale Highways Board,[3] and one month later these were ratified by the Select Committee. Chatton Road crossing was just a few yards east of a ford over the Wooler Water, and this was less than convenient for road traffic held up by the railway. The NER was very lucky not to have to provide a bridge in place of the ford when it was so close to the level crossing. Again, their solicitors evaded the problem by making an agreement to pay a mere £100 towards the cost of a bridge 'whenever it was built'. Soon after the railway opened the bridge had to be provided. With Wooler station being situated between the two important level crossings considerable hold-ups were to occur in later years when the daily shunting operations were being carried out (figure 3.3).

The route beyond Wooler presented several options, and the final choice may have been influenced by the rival Central Northumberland Railway scheme. The direct route to Cornhill via Milfield had been staked out by the NER, but was rejected apparently as it was considered that the adjacent area was already adequately served by Beal, Belford and Coldstream stations. One of the local residents was so certain that the direct route had been chosen that he even built a hotel near the tiny hamlet of Ewart to serve the rush of customers that the railway would generate! (This building still survives and is fairly obvious by its size and the lack of windows on what was to be the railway side.) In 1883 the NER produced a map, for issue to its directors and major customers, which showed the direct route to Cornhill and not the more westerly one for which it had Parliamentary Powers, and was almost ready to be let to contract!

After Wooler any alternative line had to follow the valley of the River Glen to Kirknewton and then the Bowmont Water to Mindrum Mill. Beyond Mindrum other choices of route became possible: the shortest was north-west to join the Kelso branch at either Carham or Cornhill; the next continued along the Bowmont Valley nearly to Yetholm and then skirted the spurs of the hills with some very steep gradients to Kelso; the longest was to Yetholm and Morebattle and then along the Kale Water to join the NBR about four miles west of Kelso. The Duke of Roxburghe, Lord Tankerville of Chillingham Castle, and some supporters in Wooler and Kelso preferred the longest route. The NER chose the one from Mindrum to Cornhill, but it is hard to say if this short detour was justified on economic grounds. There was a fleeting proposal for a private company to construct a line from Mindrum to Kelso via Yetholm, but the promoters soon realised the futility of the project.[4]

From Wooler through Akeld to Kirknewton the chosen route proceeds with easy gradients and minor earthworks along the level bed of a former glacial lake. The turnpike road turns northwards at Akeld and it was taken over the railway by a stone-arch bridge, which has been demolished since the line was closed. West of Kirknewton station the College Burn is crossed near the point where it joins the Bowmont Water to form the River Glen. Here the railway swings northwards into far more rugged terrain, but, with the use of heavier earthworks, the gradients are less severe than in the middle section of the branch.

The major engineering works on the second contract were between Westnewton and Kilham where the Bowmont Valley narrows. The river itself had to be diverted for about 200 yards near Kilham, and there were problems with soft ground adjacent to it. The largest cutting on this section was 45 feet deep, and was spanned by a three-arched bridge giving access to Canno Mill. A little north of Mindrum station a minor road is carried over the railway at a heavy skew, utilising 78 feet by 7 feet deep wrought-iron plate girders. From Mindrum the descent of 163 feet into the Tweed Valley has gradients no steeper than 1 in 82. This was achieved by a series of embankments 200 to 300 yards long, particularly in the last two miles near Learmouth. These had maximum heights of between 25 and 35 feet. The line joined the alignment of the Kelso branch about half-a-mile south of Coldstream station, but the actual junction was near to the platform ends.

W. W. Tomlinson, in his history of the NER, devotes a paragraph to the branch (pp. 689-90) and, surprisingly, makes no less than three mistakes. He refers to the 'immense embankment over Learmouth Bog', and gives the length of Hillhead Tunnel as 'a mile and a half long'. There is no way that this nondescript embankment, which still exists, could be called immense; the tunnel was 351 yards long. He also states that 'the attention of the Board had been directed to a somewhat neglected part of their territory by the revival of a scheme for a Central Northumberland Railway'. All evidence indicates that it was the A&C scheme that provoked the counter-proposal by the CNR.

In addition to the tunnel and viaduct there were 101 bridges and culverts on the branch; the average of three per mile was reasonable for the type of country that it passed through. Also, it was considered wise to replace a cast-iron bridge on the Kelso branch at Coldstream station by a wrought-iron one, at a cost of £372, prior to the B.O.T. inspection.[5] (Cast iron, except when used in arches, was generally distrusted following the Tay Bridge disaster in 1879.) The NER followed a fairly common practice on single lines by making the overbridges double track width. The viaduct and underbridges, except in the station areas, were single track width. The masonry overbridges were all of a segmental-arched style with a span square to the track of 30 feet (plate 3.6). The highway widths provided at over and underbridges were 12 feet, 25 feet and 35 feet for farm accesses, public roads and turnpikes respectively.

The permanent way was laid to the NER standards of that time, and comprised double-headed rails weighing 82 lbs per yard on 42 lb cast-iron chairs, which were fastened by spikes and trenails to 10 or 11 sleepers per 30 feet length of rail. The ballast appears to be a mixture of graded stone from the rock cuttings, gravel and the ash normally used by the NER at that time (plate 6.8). In all, 5,000 tons of rails were used, and the cost of the permanent way material came to £1,200 per mile.

**Plate 3.6: a typical bridge carrying a farm track over the railway. The span of the bridge was 30 feet to accommodate a second track if one was ever needed! The roadway width was 12 feet. J. F. Mallon.**

## ENDNOTES

1.      *Proceedings of I. C. E. Vol. 94*, pp. 301-313. Obituaries.
2.      Other details of the line used in this chapter are taken from the Deposited Parliamentary Plans, NER Line Diagrams and Gradient Sections.
3.      Way and Works Committee, 19 February 1882.
4.      *Newcastle Daily Journal*, 20 April 1886.
5.      Way and Works, 31 March 1887.

# CHAPTER FOUR: CONSTRUCTION

On 9 June 1883, over a year after the Act was passed, the *Alnwick Mercury* reported on the disappointment expressed by the people along the route of the railway at the delays in making a start. The paper suggested that the NER directors 'were not as blamable as some would suppose'. It pointed out that the district traversed was rough, the works heavy and the need for the large number of bridges extended the time needed to mature the plans. It expressed the hope that the line would be out to contract by the autumn.

Although the survey for the parliamentary plans had started in February 1881 the detailed survey was not completed until April 1883, and then boreholes still had to be taken to discover the subsoil conditions. In these days of electronically recorded survey data and computer aided design it is easy to forget that, even thirty years ago, it was a long and difficult process to design a new route. Now with the survey data stored in the computer it is possible, in a little time at the keyboard, to produce plots of alternative alignments and their cross sections, together with the volume of earthworks, and thus achieve the best possible compromise.

It is a daunting thought that for the Alnwick and Cornhill it was necessary to plot to scale 3,000 cross-sections derived from at least 15,000 level readings. Then the proposed formation, derived from the longitudinal gradient section, had to be drawn on each cross section in order to work out the earthwork volumes. These cross sections alone required 77 large sheets of drawings.[1] The only aid in those days was a large book of tables that had been compiled from the 1830s by a former president of the Institution of Civil Engineers, George Parker Bidder.[2] These allowed the volumes of the earthworks to be worked out more speedily.

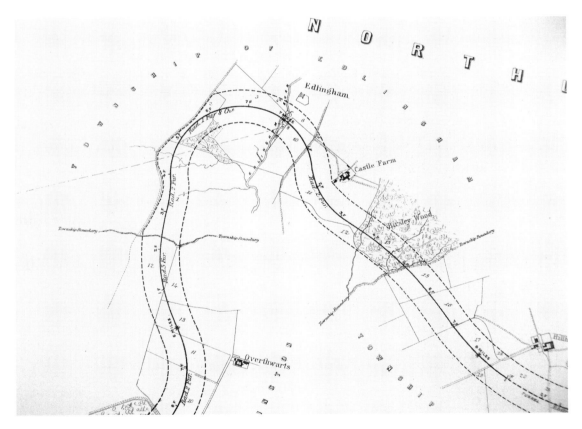

**Figure 4.1: part of the Deposited Plan for Edlingham showing the railway reversing direction 2 miles south of Summit (below bottom left) by means of an 18 chain (1188 feet) radius curve to take its northerly course to Wooler. The limit of deviation is restricted on the east side of the curve by the county road from Alnwick, now B6341**

Standard limits of deviation, of 110 yards (5 chains or 100 metres), on each side of the centre line shown on the deposited plans were permitted in rural areas, so some improvements to the gradients and curvature were always possible after the detailed survey was complete. The engineer did not only have to establish the best vertical and horizontal alignment, but he had to balance the cut and fill to avoid, where possible, hauling excavated material long distances. A lot of trial and error and many adjustments would be required.

The exact parcels of land required from each landowner were worked out by the engineer from the survey and final levels with allowances for the formation width, working margins and the slide slopes established for the cuttings and embankments. When the engineer had finalised his scheme land purchase was not a delay as the Act had granted compulsory purchase powers to the railway where needed. The Alnwick and Cornhill required just over 400 acres, giving around 11½ acres per mile, or an average width between fences of 95 feet.

During the negotiations, prior to the line being built, the NER had insisted on fair land prices as there had been many bitter experiences in the past when dealing with greedy landowners. In the 1830s the London and Birmingham Railway had had to pay an average £6,275 per mile over its 112 mile route when almost all of it was across agricultural land. Even with the agreement of 14 landowners, covering over half the land required, the purchase, compensation and legal fees for the Alnwick and Cornhill came to nearly £50,000 or in excess of £1,400 per mile. This was over 11% of the total cost of the railway. George Irving, the NER's estate agent at Newcastle, was responsible for the negotiations for the land, and he paid an average price of £120 per acre. One of the lowest prices was £30 per acre to O. C. B. Cresswell, who was very much in favour of the line, and the highest, as was to be expected, was for half-an-acre of private garden in Alnwick at a rate of £900 per acre. The largest quantity of land from any one owner, Lord Tankerville, was 68½ acres, and as one of the signatories of the agreement he sold for £4,000 [3]. The second largest area was required from an owner who was opposed to the railway, and the price had to be settled as compulsory purchase before a special jury in the Sheriff's Court at Newcastle. He asked £18,000 for 55 acres, the NER offered £4,500 and he was awarded £6,700 including compensation.[4] Arbitration nearly always reduced the compensation claimed against the company, but when the solicitor considered one fortunate tenant he was awarded £570 against the £300 that he had claimed.[5] Compensation was paid for severance, loss of timber, access, buildings, water supply, etc, and on this line amounted to £12,000.

The drawings, sections and Bill of Quantities were ready sufficiently for the NER to go out to tender in October 1883, although some of the items still had to be priced on a schedule of rates as not all the drawings were complete. For example, a number of drawings for the more complex bridges were not available for another 15 months. This delayed the signing of the Deed of Contract for them until 5 May 1885.[6] The line was divided into two separate contracts, and the results from the firms that submitted were as follows [7]: -

| Name of Contractor | Contract No 1 | Contract No 2 |
|---|---|---|
| **NER Engineer's Estimate** | **£159,239** | **£161,674** |
| G. Meakin & J. W. Dean, Hampstead | £135,862 | £136,405 |
| G. B. Godfrey, Hull | £109,750 | £114,800 |
| R. Yeaman, Felton | £156,152 | - |
| H. Lovatt, Wolverhampton | £160,000 | - |
| Walter Scott & Co., Newcastle | £163,670 | £158,087 |
| S. Pearson & Co., Bradford | £167,800 | £157,500 |
| Holme & King, Liverpool | £179,107 | £180,374 |
| T. Oliver, Horsham | £183,958 | - |
| Nowell & Snowden, Manchester | £184,000 | £200,000 |
| Easton & Gibb, Skipton | £197,232 | £186,585 |
| John Waddell, Edinburgh | £225,155 | £178,569 |
| Thomas Ridley, Middlesbrough | - | £169,500 |

The NER was not obliged to accept the lowest tender and in this case accepted Messrs. Meakin & Dean's of Hampstead as being a viable proposition, regardless of the fact it was £50,000 below its own engineer's estimate. Although, Meakin & Dean had been in railway contracting for some years, and had done work for the Highland, Midland and London & North Western Railways, as well as at Birkenhead Docks, this was the first time that they had tendered for work on the NER.

Contract No. 1 for the southern 14 miles 23 chains from Alnwick had by far the most difficult engineering works; this explains why the cost per mile was 50% greater than for Contract No. 2. Although Meakin & Dean had been awarded both contracts they ran them, in the main, as two separate jobs. They still used time-honoured methods of employing hundreds of navvies with horses working concurrently at several sites along the line. They used at least seven tank locomotives, steam and derrick cranes, but little other mechanical plant as picks, shovels and blasting powder were still the main methods of getting the work done.

Work started at the Alnwick contract on 12 January 1884: -

> 'Quietly, unostentatiously, and without any ceremony, the first sod of the deep cutting for the formation of the new line of railway between Alnwick and Cornhill, was raised on Tuesday last at Mossy Ford (NU 160110), and therefore it may be considered that the work in connection with Messrs. Meakin and Dean's heavy undertaking has now commenced.' [8]

Owing to the weather and lack of lodging accommodation for the men it did not proceed very enthusiastically, and work did not start at Wooler until mid-May.

Although T. E. Harrison reported to the NER board at the mid-1884 half-yearly meeting that 'the contract for the Alnwick & Cornhill was being carried out satisfactorily', only £25,000 had been paid for work in the first six months. The average expenditure per half-year after that was just above £60,000, but the NER had budgeted for a considerably higher rate of progress. In his half-yearly report for June 1885, with only £150,000 of work carried out, T. E. Harrison reported that there was a prospect of the line being completed by mid-1886. His report, a year later, said the work had been greatly delayed by the severe winter, and he hoped 'the contractor will now be able to carry on more expeditiously.'

George Meakin died on 31 July 1886, and at the beginning of October Mr. Dean indicated that he was unable to complete the contract.[9] The bad winters and difficulties with the rock cuttings at the southern end had contributed to his decision. Although it has been stated that Meakin & Dean went bankrupt on this contract it is not so. They were still working on the road bridge over the Tweed at Norham and at Birkenhead Docks in the following year. The completion of the line was taken over by the NER using the contractor's personnel and plant.

Although the contractors had found the work at the south end extremely difficult they had made no attempt to skimp it. An inspection by the directors just before Meakin & Dean withdrew gave the verdict the works 'were *too* well done'. Some credit must go to the NER's resident engineers, Messrs. E. B. Forbes and C. White, and the contractor's agents, J. Weston for the southern contract and P. Ayres for the other, but a lot is due to the workforce who carried out prodigious feats of earthmoving in all weathers, and often in dangerous conditions. It is only in recent years that the considerable contribution, both to the railway system and the country as a whole, has been acknowledged to the previously maligned but extremely hard working navvy (see Chapter 5).

Besides the basic earthmoving a variety of temporary and permanent works, some of a skilled or semi-skilled nature, were needed to complete the contract. Amongst those employed were; timekeepers, blacksmiths and strikers, carpenters and joiners, masons, quarry men, engine drivers and firemen, fitters, crane and mortar mill operators, horse drivers and, at the height of the works, around 2,000 labourers.

In the early stages of the contract general site clearance, fencing, the provision of temporary accommodation and workshops, rail and road accesses were the main considerations. As the work progressed bridges and buildings were constructed and temporary tracks were extended to assist the earthmoving until, finally, the drainage and ballasting of the formation and laying of the permanent way were achieved. The work was measured not only in miles and chains but all the cuttings and embankments were numbered for easy reference.

For example, for two week's work in May 1887 nineteen platelayers were paid £32 11s. 11d. for packing and lifting the permanent way and trimming the ballast from 5m 20c to 6m 20c while nine quarrymen received £22. 0s. 3d. for work in cutting No. 23.[10]

In his half-yearly report for December 1886, T. E. Harrison claimed that since the NER had taken over 'considerably more progress had been made than previously, and there was a prospect of the line being completed during the summer'. The directors and senior officers visited Wooler on a special train from Coldstream on 16 February 1887, but they made no commitment regarding the opening of that part of the line. There was some dissatisfaction by the residents at the north end of the line at the delays when to them the work seemed complete. In mid-March the people of Cornhill circulated a petition demanding the opening of the line.[11]

On 22 April the NER chairman, directors and officials were able to make their first journey through the whole line. The longest part from Alnwick to Wooler must have been somewhat uncomfortable. Not only was it made in an open wagon hauled by a small locomotive, but some of the temporary track must have been very rough as the earthworks were still incomplete. The party lunched at Wooler and then covered the rest of their journey back to Newcastle via Tweedmouth in the comfort of a train of three saloons. They decided to open the line from Cornhill (Coldstream Station) to Wooperton, for goods traffic only, on Monday 2 May.[12] They hoped that the whole line would be opened for all traffic by the beginning of August. This was not to be as the construction difficulties at the southern end, which had bedevilled the contractor's efforts, were to delay the opening for another month.

**Plate 4.1: a historic photograph showing the Manning Wardle 0-4-0ST locomotive *Cornhill,* and some of the party that travelled on the first journey to inspect the whole line on 22 April 1887. The locomotive was purchased new by Meakin & Dean in 1884, and towards the end of its working life was used by Walter Scott & Co. on the Great Central Railway's London Extension. Courtesy of the Glendale History Society.**

During May 1887 the weekly wages bill still exceeded £1,000, and around 800 men were employed on Contract No. 1. Over half the men were still carrying out earthworks, while the remainder were finishing the buildings and bridges and laying and ballasting the permanent way.[13] Again, in order to assess a possible opening date for the whole line, a party of 22 directors and officers made a journey through from Cornhill to Alnwick on Wednesday 6

June. They were accompanied by the Earl and Countess of Tankerville, of Chillingham Castle, from Wooler to Ilderton. After noting the outstanding work it was considered that it would be impossible to open at the beginning of August for passenger traffic.[14] A suggestion to open the remainder of the line from Wooperton to Alnwick for goods traffic was rejected as it was realised that the passage of the trains would hamper the completion of the works. The beginning of September was the best estimate for completion, and the necessary one month's notice, required by the B.O.T, was given for the inspection necessary prior to the opening of the branch for passengers.[15]

In mid-August, just before Major-General Hutchinson (1826-1912) commenced his B.O.T inspection, some signalling work was incomplete, and was actually still going on 'day and night' during his tour. It was not known as late as 26 August when the line would be opened to traffic. A last minute alarm occurred when some initial settlement of the piers was noticed during the inspection of Edlingham Viaduct, but it was not considered to need any remedial work.[16] Everyone concerned must have breathed a sigh of relief when it was announced that the passenger service could commence on Monday 5 September. At last the line could start to earn revenue some 18 months later than anticipated at the outset.

Following the opening there were one or two minor slips in the raw earthworks, but in general everything worked well. By 1 December the line was in good enough shape for its maintenance to be taken over by the NER district engineer's lengthmen appointed to the branch. The 80 remaining former contractor's men, that had been retained to carry out the heavy packing and lining of the track during its initial settling down under traffic, were paid-off on 30 November.[17]

Meakin & Dean's plant was disposed of in two auctions on the instructions of the NER board. The first, held after the completion of No. 2 Contract, had items for sale at Cornhill, Mindrum, Wooler and Wooperton. The very first passenger train was to take prospective buyers from Coldstream to Wooperton stopping en route; it ran on 8 June 1887.[18] The remainder of the plant was auctioned at Alnwick on 26 and 27 October; included were seven hand-derrick and five steam cranes, 150 three cubic yard spoil wagons, scrap rails and seven tank locomotives of various makes. The locomotives were: *Sambo, Frank, Belsize, Wanderer, Hebburn, Cornhill* and *No. 2*.

T. E. Harrison's last half-yearly report made on 24 January 1888, just one month before he died, stated that the line 'was working satisfactorily.' The total cost of the engineering works was £376,811, and the total for the branch, including land and legal costs, was £437,664, comfortably within the £500,000 allowed by its Act. The figure of £12,330 per mile compared favourably with NER's single line from Leyburn to Hawes, completed in 1878, which cost £13,500. The Midland Railway's extension from Hawes to the Settle and Carlisle cost an astronomical £40,000 per mile!

## ENDNOTES

1.      PRO RAIL 527/2306-12.
2.      G. P. Bidder (1806-1878) was father of the Q.C. of the same name at the Select Committee hearing.
3.      Way and Works (WW) 6 December 1883.
4.      WW 19 June 1884.
5.      WW 17 December 1885.
6.      PRO RAIL 527/629.
7.      WW 6 December 1883.
8.      *Alnwick Gazette, (AG)* 16 January 1884.
9.      Ibid. 9 October 1886.
10.     PRO RAIL 527/1092.
11.     *AG,* 19 March 1887.
12.     *AG,* 30 April & 7 May 1887.
13.     PRO RAIL 527/1092.
14.     *AG,* 9 July 1887.
15.     WW 21 July 1887. The opening of the north end of the line to freight in May had not required a Board of Trade inspection.
16.     *AG,* 27 August 1887.
17.     PRO RAIL 527/1092, WW 17 November 1887.
18.     *AG,* 11 June 1887.

## CHAPTER FIVE: THE NAVVIES by Vera Mallon.

The history of the railway would be incomplete without reference to the men who built it, the staff who worked the line and the people who used it (see Chapter 8).

An abbreviation of the term 'navigator' was used to describe the labourers who were employed in the building of canals, docks, roads and railways. Early in 1884 the first of hundreds of 'navvies' started to arrive in the area between Alnwick and Whittingham, with the greatest numbers concentrated in the Alnwick district. The town, with its population of less than 8,000 was already overcrowded, and had experienced an influx of navvies some 30 years earlier during the building of the old railway station and the branch to it from Bilton (Alnmouth). A report on the increase in population in Alnwick parish between 1841 and 1851, after the construction of the local railways, suggested that 'no doubt a considerable number of Irish located themselves in the place, but not in sufficient numbers to explain the increase.' [1] After the start of the Alnwick and Cornhill contract the chairman of the Alnwick Local Board of Health expressed his concern about 'the influx of labourers consequent on the carrying out of the railway works'. He said he knew for a fact that 'the other evening, 95 navvies had been seen coming into the town through Clayport Street. When they were added to those who were employed at Dunterns and the wagon ways they got an idea of the additional population that the town housed at the present time'.

Navvies had a reputation for being physically strong, rough, tough and very hard working – characteristics which enabled them to endure the conditions in which they laboured. They also earned a reputation for being quarrelsome and unruly in their place of work, and for disorderly behaviour in the community. The army of men that worked on the A&C would be no exception. It would be surprising if problems did not exist when men of different ages, nationalities and backgrounds not only worked together, but were required to live at very close quarters in a difficult or even hostile environment. When construction began in mid-January 1884, it was a time of foul weather with storm force winds, hail, sleet, snow and frosts. In early February 'a hurricane blew down upwards of 1,000 trees in Hulne Park [Alnwick]'.

Temporary wooden structures to serve as houses for the workmen had been erected on the bank of the Black Burn, just west of Mossy Ford (NU 160111). Huts for workmen and offices for the engineers and clerks were built in the vicinity of Glanton and Hedgeley. In April, a press report stated:

> 'During the past months many difficulties have presented themselves – not only in the nature of the work to be done in the neighbourhood of Rugley [NU 168106], Mossy Ford, Lemmington Hill Head [NU 107108] and other places, but in the unfavourable period of the year for such work, and the obtaining of labour or rather the want of accommodation for the men employed. In the latter respect many changes we understand have taken place; for in the outlying districts, men who came to engage in the work found it impossible to procure lodgings, and in many cases, after lying out all night, they determined to throw up the work and go in search of fresh fields of labour. A number of huts, it is true, were erected for the men but these, it would appear, failed to meet all requirements, and the offer of lodgings, as it were, at the various villages was not equal to the demand.'

One reason for the lack of village accommodation may be seen in the comment of the late Mrs. Diamond, born in Glanton in 1879, who later recalled; 'When we heard that the navvies were seeking lodgings in the village we were full of fear, having heard so much of the rough Irishmen on this job'. She went on to say that; 'When they came, they were quiet and inoffensive, and apart from making their merry presence felt in the village local on a Saturday night, it was as if they had never come'. Many more examples of this different picture of the navvies and their acceptance in the local communities are recorded.

It is often thought that the navvies were Irish, but in general the majority were English. However, there was a high percentage on this line with a Celtic background, particularly Welshmen, and it is likely that a number were Scotsmen due to the proximity of the Border.

The lack of accommodation, the weather, the nature of the work and the arduous terrain were not the only difficulties encountered by the navvies. At the beginning of May 1884: -

'The blacksmiths and carpenters together with their labourers, employed on the Alnwick section, struck for a reduction of six hours a week, they having been working an average rate of 10 hours per day. A few men returned to work, remaining on their original terms. The vacancies created by those who left were filled by new employees who agreed to the contractor's conditions'.

Although there were inns and taverns in the towns and some of the villages on the route of the railway, the men working in remote areas were less well served. The Shepherd's Rest at the top of Clayport, in Alnwick, was not too distant from the sites at Greensfield [NU 189119] and Rugley. The nearest public house to the workings on the west of Alnwick Moor was the Ravensworth Arms at Learchild, built when the new road was constructed. Known previously as both the Swinburne Arms and the Buston Arms, the licensed victualler was Maria Shanks. It was said that the inn was frequented by Irish labourers working on the railway, and they regarded the landlord's daughter as a witch. According to legend, whenever she served drinks, it did not matter what coin she was given in payment, she always had the correct change ready in her hand.

The chairman of the bench at the Alnwick Petty Sessions understood the men's need for alcoholic refreshments. Men described as a hut-keeper, a ganger, a horse-keeper and a labourer were charged with selling beer and whisky without a licence at Mossy Ford after a member of the Northumbrian Constabulary 'having the garb of a navvy, visited the defendants' huts' where he saw alcoholic liquor supplied and money received. The chairman referred to the fact that it was 2½ miles from town, and it was desirable that men who were navvies – men who were 'here today and gone tomorrow' – should have a reasonable supply of drink in the place where they worked in order that they may be kept at their work, which would, perhaps, not be the case were the men to come into town. He went on to say that 'the water at that place was not very clear nor very palatable', and for those reasons he asked the bench to impose as lenient a fine as possible. This proved to be £5 and costs.

**Plate 5.1: the 'Pavilion Inn' built to serve the navvies near Hillhead Tunnel. J. F. Mallon collection.**

One hut-keeper, Mr. Limb, was granted a licence for both beer and spirits, and his establishment, near Hillhead Tunnel, became known as 'The Pavilion Inn' – also referred to by a visiting reporter as 'Pavilion Hotel'. When another hut-keeper's application for licence to sell alcohol on his premises on Alnwick Moor was heard at Alnwick, it was opposed by the

Temperance Council. Mr. Hindmarsh, an Alnwick solicitor appearing for the applicant, referred to the large number of men working in the vicinity of Alnwick, and the laborious nature of their work. He declared that the men often required stimulants, and that it was the general custom. He felt it wiser to keep the men on the Moor rather than 'wandering through the town'. He supported his contention by reminding the bench that the hut-keepers would have more control over the men 'in checking the indulgence of any of the excesses which men once got into a public house were apt to indulge in', and that the place would be open to police supervision.

Mr. Robinson, a Newcastle solicitor acting for the Alnwick Temperance Council, opposed the case on the grounds that the licence was not necessary since there were only 60 men in that place, and that there was another public house within half-a-mile. In his support, the Navvy Missionary declared that the men 'did not desire this additional temptation to be put in their way, their feelings were decidedly against it'.

The bench decided in favour with the only condition that the applicant, Thomas Oxenham, kept a room for the sole purpose of those who purchased drink. It is thought that this hut became known as 'The Railway Hotel'. Another pub was known as the 'Garden of Eden'.

In December 1884, Sir John Swinburne M.P. (a CNR supporter), asked the NER for an assurance that it would take the necessary steps to close the public houses in the vicinity of his estates on expiry of their licences in the summer of 1885. This the company agreed to.[2]

Despite the increase in licensed premises, liquor still continued to be sold illegally. Two incidents were recorded where police attempting to serve summonses on some navvies for the offence were severely beaten up. At Lumby Law, near Edlingham, a sergeant was set about, knocked to the ground and kicked by the hut-keeper and other navvies. Another navvy remonstrated with them 'shouting you are not going to commit murder', and 'sat over the victim's head to protect him'. When the group departed the Good Samaritan sought medical assistance for the victim. The ringleader, who had worked as a mason on the railway, was arrested in Derbyshire and given 'the heaviest fine of six months hard labour'.

An incident of a different kind occurred in 1886. The local Police Superintendent was driving a trap on Alnwick Moor when 'a navvy in a white smock suddenly came on to the road, and startled the horse, which bolted and threw the Superintendent out of the trap.' He suffered severe injuries to his back and head.

The men were paid fortnightly, and over half their wages went to pay off 'subs' or debts incurred, so when short of money and hungry the navvies indulged in poaching. When a shepherd at Greensfield told the poachers to desist, he was stoned and inflicted with 'severe injuries' before the men ran off. The perpetrator, perhaps the most accurate shot, was apprehended later and fined 50 shillings (£2-50). When unable to pay he was committed to gaol for a month. Captain Noble, the tenant of Castle Farm, Edlingham, claimed, unsuccessfully, £150 from the NER for the cost of an extra gamekeeper during the construction of the line.[3] Poaching continued despite the gamekeepers using a 'very bright searchlight', which could 'awaken residents on the edge of town [Alnwick]'.

In 1886 serious charges of 'Abduction and Larceny' were made against a young foreman-navvy. Reuben Jones was accused of stealing bed clothes and linen from a hut-keeper, James Holtman. He was also charged with taking away Holtman's under 16 year-old daughter, Emma, 'without the consent of her father or mother'. On 17 August 1886 Jones was arrested on the 2-35pm train at Alnwick station. He was accompanied by Emma, her mother and the boxes of allegedly stolen linen. In court, Holtman admitted that, after a row on the previous evening, Emma had left *under her mother's control, and was still with her* on the train when Jones was arrested. It was also accepted that the linen was Mrs. Holtman's, so the case was dismissed. The young couple were married on 14 September.

One navvy found a means of reducing his expenses by producing counterfeit florins (10p coins) and using them to pay for his lodgings. These aroused suspicion, so he was committed first to the local prison, and then for trial at Newcastle on the charge of rendering counterfeit florins and the possession of a mould for casting them.

Not all the stories about the navvies that reached the local newspapers were to their detriment, nor was their welfare neglected. The Bishop of Newcastle promoted a special mission for the navvies, and in his appeal for support he wrote: -

'The formation of the line of railway between Alnwick and Cornhill has led to the employment of a large number of workmen who are scattered about a somewhat inaccessible part of the country. Experience has shown the need of an organised effort to supply men working under such conditions with religious teaching. I undertook the responsibility of appointing a Missioner for the special purpose of visiting the navvies, and trying to bring home the truths of the Gospel.'

The Rev. J. S. Phillips, who took up these duties on 24 April 1884, recorded: -

'It was a strange parish, about 20 yards in width, and 35 miles in length. Since that time I have made 61 journeys along it, of one, two and sometimes three days each. The first thing started was the Saturday night entertainment at Alnwick, which was carried out all summer with great success. The men are kept out of temptation to drink, and are educated and civilised by hearing good music, singing and suitable readings. In the season of Advent we had special services which were well attended. I have preached over 100 sermons at regular services in churches, missions and schoolrooms, in addition to sermons and addresses in huts, Bible classes and Temperance meetings…. The details of the work, such as writing letters after missing friends and relations, private talkings with the men, and the 1001 things which occur in mission work it is impossible to describe. There are regular services every weekend at Alnwick, every Sunday at Edlingham, and occasionally along the line. There are many discouragements. The temptation to drink, men too tired to listen – sometimes rebuffs – the extreme length of the line, the distance of huts from one another, making it hard to centralise the work. These and other causes have told against the work, but as an old missioner said the other day, one benefit of the work is that it witnesses to the care which the Church of England tries to take to all sorts and conditions of men.'

The Rev. Phillips was replaced by the Rev. J. H. Rudkin at the beginning of 1886, and other local clergymen continued to support the Mission. In an article on Edlingham in a local paper it was written that: -

'The population of the village is by the influence of the navvies, temporarily increased. These "hardy sons of toil" have the sympathy of the vicar bestowed upon them in no small degree. That worthy gentleman has kindly granted them the use of the schoolroom after school hours as a reading room. He has moreover provided seats, tables, window curtains, lamps, spittoons and writing materials; and members of his family and friends have supplied bagatelle, chess, dominoes etc. and daily and weekly papers and periodicals are also kindly donated. This kindly interest in their welfare is reciprocated by the navvies in the pleasing and kindly manner with which they accord respect to the vicar.'

This was fairly typical: further north at Chillingham, the seat of the Earl of Tankerville, an Alnwick reporter found: -

'…there were the navvies' weekday and Sunday visitations, preachings, meat teas, and the establishment of a reading room built by the Earl of Tankerville for the use of the navvies on the Wooler railway. We also understand that Mr. Bryant, of the estates office in Chillingham, will give educational classes to the navvies as well as the young working lads at Chillingham during the winter months'.

The Alnwick and Cornhill Navvies' Mission Fund was paid for by donations from the Anglican Church, the contractors, major landowners and local residents. There seemed to be as much emphasis on providing entertainment and leisure facilities for the navvies as there was on the evangelical side. Everything from cricket matches with local teams to the navvies' attendance at the major events in the Church's liturgical calendar are reported in the local papers, and indicate an integration with the local society not to be found in earlier accounts of railway contracts.

The men had little regard for safety and numerous accidents occurred during the course of the works. It has been said that one man was killed for every mile of railway constructed in Britain. The Alnwick & Cornhill was by no means one of the worst, but it certainly had one man killed or maimed for each mile of its length. Some, like the man who was killed by falling off a locomotive he should not have been on, or the navvy who jumped from a fast moving train to retrieve his cap, and broke his leg, cannot be accorded the same sympathy as a worker who was carrying out his duties correctly and was killed or maimed by the actions of others. Most accidents were caused by falls of earth or rock in the excavations or being crushed or run over by vehicles. Even before the NER took over from the contractor it showed some benevolence by employing men disabled on the line on light duties elsewhere on its system, such as gatekeepers, when they were fit to return to work.[4]

The number of men seriously injured on the line was causing financial problems for Alnwick Infirmary. At its annual committee meeting, on 15 October 1884, it was reported that 11 of the 50 in-patients, treated in the year, 'were men connected with the Alnwick and Cornhill Railway, and their share of the expenditure amounts to £40, the only additional sum received on account thereof, being a subscription of £5-5s (£5.25) from Messrs. Meakin and Dean.' It was felt that the contractors had a duty 'under the Employer's Liability Act to pay for the injured man's maintenance'. It was resolved:-

> 'That the contractors and sub-contractors of the new line be written to, asking them for a contribution to the funds to meet the increased outlay during the past year.'

> 'That the contractors and sub-contractors be informed, that in case of admission to the Infirmary being sought by men in their employ, any vacant accommodation shall be afforded on payment of the expenses, and otherwise subject to the rules of the Institution.'

The contractors did not comply, as on 21 March 1885 a navvy with several broken ribs was refused admission to the infirmary twice over a space of two hours, and was forced to seek lodgings. The *Gazette* commented: 'No provision whatever is made by them [the contractors] for accidents that are continually occurring on the railway. This should not be so. I am not aware of the men contracting themselves out of the Employer's Liability Act.' There were no further cases of men being refused admission, so the contractors must have paid up.

One dangerous incident that did not result in serious injuries happened on 31 July 1886. The brakes failed on a contractor's train made up of a locomotive and six wagons containing a number of navvies. The speed was so great that on its approach to Alnwick it failed to negotiate the curve at the new junction with the branch from Alnmouth where it derailed, and the wreckage blocked the junction. Fortunately, a passenger train, due a minute or two later, was stopped before it ran into it.[5]

Descriptions of the workmen's huts indicate that around 20 men could be accommodated in each. One of the huts was described as having seven rooms built for the inmates, and two public rooms. In 1886, a reporter from the *Newcastle Daily Journal* visited the workings, and saw 'neat, clean and spacious' huts along the line, beginning with what was known as 'Shanty Charlie's' at Alnwick, where work on the new station had just commenced. The hundreds of men occupying the huts were described as 'big, brawny, rough-hewn fellows. Most of them were Welshmen or men who had worked on railways or other contract work in Wales'. Around this time there were said to be some 700 men working on the southern sector, and 600 in the northern end beyond Wooperton.

It is known that some of the men had families with them. Glanton school records show that in June 1887 there were 116 children on the school roll, but in August it was written that; 'Attendance is very low, children from the new railway workings have left'.

Other children were missing from the school rolls, which resulted in a recommendation that the school attendance officer should 'explore that portion of the district where some of the railway huts were erected, where he would see numbers of children running about all day'. Also, he should 'pay a visit of inspection to a few of the outsiders, and I fancy he will find many truants, who have for sometime been running wild'. It is not recorded if these measures were effective.

Those navvies living in lodgings were likely to have their meals provided, and it may be thought that hut-keepers provided meals for their residents. However, a letter sent to the editor of the *Newcastle Daily Journal* on 20 May 1887, from a navvy working at Lemmington Bank, indicates that the age-old racketeering on contracts still persisted: -

'I hope you will find space for the following few facts of how we navvies are treated on the Alnwick and Cornhill Railway. After getting a start, we must go to a hut to lodge, where we have to buy everything we want from the owner of the hut. Butterine is sold to us at 1s per lb, which can be bought for 6d per lb; and we are not allowed to take fresh butter. Box eggs are sold to us at 1d each, which can be bought for 6d per dozen; American bacon we pay 9d for, which is generally sold at 4d per lb, sugar we pay 3d for which is not fit to use, tobacco we must buy the very worst quality; and beer which is unfit for anyone to drink. Shirts, stockings and everything we use we must buy from the hut-keeper. We are not allowed to take in a pound of butcher meat unless we buy it from the hut-keeper. One man brought it in, but he had to leave the hut, throw the bacon away, or eat it uncooked, which he did. That is only one case out of many which I could give you. As to their having licences to sell beer and tobacco, I am not interested, but I think if the directors of the NER company knew how we were treated they would put a stop to it.'

A week later this letter was copied in the *Alnwick and County Gazette,* and it brought a response from Thomas Oxenham, who, it will be remembered, had been granted a licence to sell alcohol in his hut. In 1884 he had narrowly evaded bankruptcy, but was still in business, and used the navvy's letter to argue the case in the paper for hut-keepers, like himself, who were not gangers on the railway: -

'There is some truth in the letter – for it happened in a hut not eight miles from Alnwick. Of course men are compelled to lodge with a ganger if they are working for him, but if the North-Eastern Railway Company, or any other company, would not allow their gangers to keep huts, they would get better men who would stay longer. As it is, if a dirty, filthy man who has been refused lodging by a ganger, comes to a hut, he is taken in by some poorer hut-keeper, who has no option but to take him in. Then when the man gets nice and clean, and the ganger is short of lodgers, that poor fellow must go to the ganger to lodge or else get the sack.'

'I am aware that men do not stay with a ganger for long, for neither the ganger or his wife try to please them, but the hut-keeper who is not a ganger must try and keep them and please them.'

He went on to argue that the prices were not as bad as they had been presented, and at his hut 'the men fetch their own eggs from the farm and butter if they choose.' It should be borne in mind that after the NER took over the contract the average weekly wage was £1-5s (£1.25), and they charged 7s-6d (37½p) for a week's lodging, which must have included food.[6]

On the whole the railway was completed satisfactorily, if a little late, and many of the navvies must have left with fond memories of the district and its people.

## ENDNOTES

1.  *Alnwick Journal* Census Report. May 1871.
2.  Way and Works (WW) 6 January 1885.
3.  WW 10 August 1885.
4.  *Alnwick Gazette*, 6 December 1884.
5.  Ibid. 7 August 1886.
6.  PRO RAIL 527/1092.

**CHAPTER SIX: STATIONS AND TRAFFIC FACILITIES**

On 1 October 1873 Cornhill station had been renamed Coldstream after the larger and much better known Scottish town that it also served. Confusion about the name of the branch lasted throughout its life. It was officially known both as the Alnwick and Cornhill and the Alnwick and Coldstream. The line was authorised under the title 'NER Alnwick & Cornhill Act', and in many internal documents that name was used right up to its closure, but in virtually all timetables and documents available to the public it was referred to as 'Alnwick and Coldstream'. It was referred to locally as the 'Wooler line' or the 'west line', and the newspapers preferred Cornhill to Coldstream.

The ten intermediate stations on the line were named Edlingham, Whittingham, Glanton, Hedgeley, Wooperton, Ilderton, Wooler, Akeld, Kirknewton and Mindrum. The mileage of all the stations and signal cabins is given in Appendix 1. There was some uncertainty, and a little lack of logic, about the choice of some of the station names. The architect's drawing called Ilderton 'Lilburn' and Hedgeley 'Low Hedgely [sic]'. The Traffic Committee minutes of 4 March 1886 called the latter 'Powburn' after the village that it is situated beside. On 29 April 1886 the same committee refused a request by Mr. George Culley, a CNR supporter, to name Ilderton either 'Lilburn Tower', 'Lilburn' or 'West Lilburn', but on 1 July resolved that Powburn be changed to Hedgeley.[1] A glance at the Ordnance Survey map will show that Mr. Culley's request was reasonable, but the change from Powburn to Hedgeley was not. The population figures also give weight to this view.

Details of the population served and the tickets issued for each station in the year 1901 are given in Chapter 7. Since 1883 requests had been made for an additional station at Kilham and in 1886, as a last attempt, a memorial was forwarded to the NER through Lord Tankerville for this facility.[2] It was again refused but limited siding accommodation was provided there. Interpolation of the traffic figures indicates that at best Kilham would have a maximum passenger potential of 1,500 passenger journeys per annum, and these would have robbed Mindrum's total by a similar amount. In no way could the cost of Kilham station and its staff be justified, and for once in this story commercial logic prevailed.

With the total population served by the intermediate stations being only 7,800, and an optimistic expectancy of around eight journeys per head per annum, there was not going to be a great deal of passenger traffic. (see Chapter 7) Except for Wooler, the stations on the branch booked an average of only two tickets for each train that ran; Wooler managed around seven passengers per train.

Regardless of their traffic potential the stations were elegant and substantial. In 1886 the *Newcastle Daily Journal* described them; 'For beauty completeness and substantial character they compare most favourably with any other buildings of a kindred nature on the NER system.' Praise has been lavished on them ever since and they have been described as: 'some of the finest country stations built anywhere in Britain', and 'by far the most impressive country stations built by the NER.' Why were they so elegant? It could be suggested that it was to please the major landowners or to show the NBR how railway stations should be built in rural Northumberland. Both of these may have had a minor influence, but the landowners should have been grateful to have got the line at all and have had no grumbles if the NER had copied the Rothbury branch and provided basic timber station buildings.

The stations were the work of the NER's own architect, William Bell (1844-1919), and were the result of a development in station styles dating back to the 1830s. The NER constituents had employed professional architects from private practices to design its buildings, and some first class results had emanated, for example, from G. T. Andrews and John and Benjamin Green. However, from its formation, in 1854, the NER had become unique, amongst the railways of that time, by deciding to employ its own full time architect. Bell was the railway's fourth architect and ran the department from 1877 until his retirement in 1914. In his early years he modified and used the larger of the two standard station types developed by the first NER architect, Thomas Prosser.[3] In 1885 Bell introduced his own attractive design for a similar sized two-storey building, and these were used at Byers Green and Coundon, in brick, and with stone facing on the A&C. Half-hipped roofs, mullioned windows and large verandahs were the main features, and the design may owe its inspiration to E. G. Paley's attractive station of 1864 for Grange-over-Sands on the Furness Railway.

**Plate 6.1: the NER arranged to have the stations and other features photographed when the line opened. The plates in this chapter dated 1887 are from the originals. Here we see the platform side of Wooperton station buildings in 1887. NERA.**

**Plate 6.2: Edlingham, shown here, and Kirknewton were of this design. The separate stationmaster's house is in the middle the picture, with some of the contractor's plant still spanning the wall to its right. The signal cabin was standard to the branch. 1887.**

The standard stone-faced two-storey buildings (plate 6.1, 6.6, figs.6.2, 6.3) were used at Glanton, Hedgeley, Wooperton, Ilderton, Akeld and Mindrum and an enlarged version was provided at Wooler. The standard buildings could be either right or left hand in arrangement and cost £1,686 each. Wooler, together with its waiting shed on the up platform, cost £2,856 (plates 6.4, 6.5, 6.11). At Edlingham and Kirknewton the single storey station offices shown in (plate 6.2, fig.6.4) were used and a separate stationmaster's house was provided at each at a lower total cost of £1,470. Whittingham (plate 6.3, fig. 6.5), the second most important station on the line, was unique on the NER in having an island platform on a single line railway. Its station buildings were similar to those used by Bell at Grangetown, near Middlesbrough, and Southcoates, near Hull. Whittingham platform buildings cost £1,597 and the stationmaster's house a further £398 - the same as the houses at Kirknewton and Edlingham.

**Plate 6.3: Whittingham island platform buildings looking north, also showing the water tank and signal box. J. W. Armstrong 1953.**

**Plate 6.4: Wooler looking south showing the enlarged accommodation provided. 1887.**

**Plate 6.5: the approach side of Wooler. The increased length of the single-storey building is apparent when compared with Wooperton shown below. NERA 1887.**

**Plate 6.6: the approach side of Wooperton station. The small awning at the booking office entrance was added as an afterthought at a cost of £7. The hipped-roofed lime cells can be seen at the right of the picture adjoining the coal cells. NERA 1887.**

The stone for the buildings and bridges at the northern end was from Twizell and Doddington quarries, the former being conveniently close to the NER Kelso branch. Meakin and Dean entered into a private siding agreement with the NER to enable them to load and transport the stone from Twizell station yard. Much of the stone for the southern end of the railway and the new Alnwick station came from the cuttings near the summit on Alnwick Moor. A visitor to the line in October 1886 remarked on '...the solid blocks of freestone being laboriously cut and dressed for building purposes...' in Lemmington cutting. Chocolate and cream glazing tiles were used extensively inside the waiting rooms and other areas used by the public. The exterior woodwork of the buildings was painted in similar colours.

The siding arrangements at each station are given at the end of Chapter 7. Three types of goods warehouse were used on the line and, in accordance with normal NER practice, the facilities for freight handling were varied to suit the anticipated traffic. Wooler had a large covered '7-wagon warehouse' and Whittingham and Mindrum '4-wagon warehouses' as described in the contract (the length of an average wagon was regarded as being 21 feet). Edlingham and Kirknewton had goods storage incorporated within the station buildings. Wooler cost £3,552 (plate 6.7); Whittingham and Mindrum cost £1,232 (plate 6.12, fig. 6.6). Akeld, Glanton, Hedgeley, Ilderton and Wooperton each got the '2-wagon warehouse' at a cost of £387 (plate 6.13, fig. 6.7).[4]

**Plate 6.7: Wooler's 7-wagon goods warehouse at the time that the line was opened. A class E 0-6-0T, introduced in 1886, can be seen above the wall on the right. NERA 1887.**

The stone-faced weigh office (plate 6.8 and fig. 6.8) cost £192. The one from Glanton has achieved fame by being re-erected at Beamish Open Air Museum. Coal depots were provided at every station and covered lime cells at all but Edlingham. Loading and cattle docks were built for each station and at Kilham Sidings. The dock accommodation at Wooler had to be considerably extended around 1900 to cater for the peak seasonal cattle and sheep traffic. To complete the facilities, five one-ton and four two-ton hand-cranes were ordered from Messrs. Cowans, Sheldon for use at the eight larger stations (there were two warehouse cranes at Wooler); their total cost was £320.[5]

Originally, 47 standard stone-faced cottages were built throughout the branch as detached, semi-detached or terraced dwellings for the use of railway staff, and their cost was around £350 each (plate 8.3). A cottage included a sitting room, kitchen, scullery and three bedrooms. A house for the permanent way inspector was provided at Wooler for £384. In February 1888, the clerk to the Whittingham Local Board complained that the gate at Low Learchild level crossing was kept locked, and that the key was kept at a farm house about a mile-and-a-half from the crossing. The Way and Works Committee resolved: 'That without admitting the crossing to be a public crossing, a platelayers cottage be built close to the crossing so that the key to the gate may be kept there.' As this was after Meakin & Dean had withdrawn, the contract for building this cottage was let to Drydon & Sons of Glanton for £323.[6]

**Plate 6.8: the standard weigh office and the stationmaster's house at Kirknewton. The track is laid with 82lb/yard rails on well graded stone ballast. NERA 1887.**

The first Alnwick station, dating from the opening of its branch in 1850, was a small, very basic stone structure with limited waiting facilities. In January 1884, within days of the contractors starting work on the line, the Alnwick Board of Health, having achieved its main ambition, now raised the question of a better station for Alnwick. By March the councillors had enlisted the support of the Duke of Northumberland and Earl Percy to get either a new station or considerable improvements to the existing one. Their preference was for a new station, leaving the 34 year old one for conversion into a goods depot. In May it seemed that the NER was in favour of the idea, and by December William Bell had shown outline plans to the Local Board. However, on 22 January 1885 the NER Traffic Committee turned down the proposal for a new station. They felt that any improvement should be carried out at the main line junction station of Bilton (Alnmouth) even though its passenger revenue was one-third of Alnwick's. Some lobbying must have been going on, and there was a conflict to be resolved about the road leading to the workhouse. A letter from Joseph Snowball, the Duke of Northumberland's agent, appeared in the *Alnwick Gazette* for 2 April 1885. As the Duke's agent he dealt directly with T. E. Harrison as Engineer-in-Chief rather than William Bell, the architect: -

> 'I refer to your letter of 7th ultimo referring to the road leading past the station being in abeyance as some difference of opinion existed between the directors of the NER in respect of Mr. Harrison's plan for the new station at Alnwick. Mr. Harrison now asked me to see him on Tuesday last and gave me much pleasure, as anyone interested in the town will have, to hear from him, at a meeting held in York last week, the directors had fully approved Mr. Harrison's plan with some slight modification. Therefore, when this plan is being carried out the roadway past the workhouse can be more effectively improved.'

On 5 March 1885 the architect had submitted two plans for Alnwick station to another NER Committee – this time the Way and Works – one was for architectural works costing £6,500 and the other for £11,500. On 22 March the Traffic Committee meeting, referred to in Mr. Snowball's letter, favoured the more expensive scheme and resolved that further plans and estimates should be prepared for improving the junction station at Bilton. Finally, on 3 September 1885, the Way and Works Committee agreed to accept William Bell's estimate of £11,500 for the architectural works at Alnwick based on Meakin and Dean's schedule of rates for the branch. Figure 6.1 reproduces Meakin & Dean's letter of 27 August 1885 commenting on the 'remarkably small' profit margin given by their schedule of prices. This was a valid point as the schedule had not been intended for buildings of this size. However, the contract was not awarded to Meakin & Dean until 6 March 1886 – just seven months before they formally withdrew from the railway.

**Plate 6.9: the western side of the new three-span trainshed at Alnwick in 1887. NERA.**

The new Alnwick station (plate 6.9) was to be an expensive project as, besides the architectural work, the whole station area had to be remodelled, and the total including permanent way, earthworks, bridges, road diversions and signalling was over £20,000. By contrast, North Shields, which handled ten times as many passengers per annum with three times the receipts of Alnwick, had to wait another four years to have its modified 1839 station replaced at a cost of £10,500. But North Shields' passengers were mainly workmen whereas a list of annual visitors to Alnwick Castle read like *Burke's Peerage*. The cost of the alterations at Alnwick together with the other station buildings on the branch came to over £70,000, which was more than three-quarters of the *total* cost of the Rothbury Branch. Full details and drawings of the old and new Alnwick stations appear in the late Ken Hoole's *North Eastern Branch Line Termini* (OPC 1985).

William Bell used a new style of signal cabin with gable-ends (plate 6.2, fig. 6.8) in preference to the characteristic hipped roof types that were being used throughout the Northern Division of the NER. Twenty-one of these new style cabins were used on the line to control stations and level crossings. An additional non-standard type was provided for the small passing loop at Summit (see page 92 plate 10.2). Again expense was no object as cabins were provided at many places where ground frames would have been used in similar circumstances on other branch lines. In the gate cabins only six levers were needed, and considering that the ratio for the whole of the NER was a cabin to every one-and-a-half route miles it did do rather well for a single line rural branch! Unsurprisingly, the signalling arrangements were the first to be targeted in economy measures, when the signal cabins at five of the stations along the branch were replaced by dwarf frames placed in extensions to the stations' verandahs (see page 91). The cabins were not demolished when they fell into disuse, and a few survive to this day as holiday accommodation (plate 10.8). The signalling is fully discussed in Chapter 10.

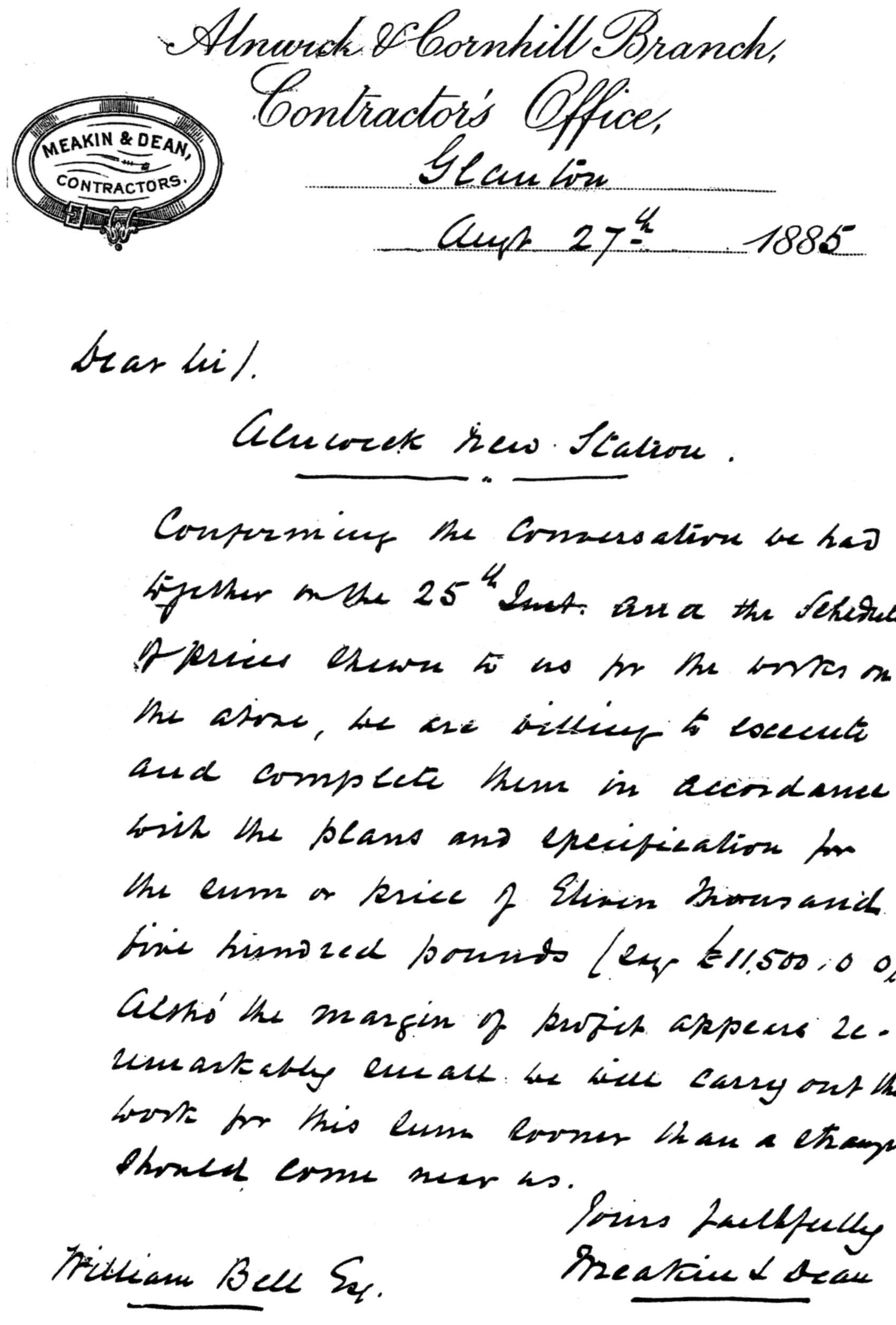

*Alnwick & Cornhill Branch,*
*Contractor's Office,*
*Glanton*
*Aug 27th 1885*

Dear Sir,

### Alnwick New Station.

Confirming the Conversation we had together on the 25th Inst. and the Schedule of prices shewn to us for the works on the above, we are willing to execute and complete them in accordance with the plans and specification for the sum or price of Eleven Thousand five hundred pounds (say £11,500 . 0 . 0). Altho' the margin of profit appears un-remarkably small we will carry out the work for this sum sooner than a stranger should come near us.

Yours faithfully
Meakin & Dean

William Bell Esq.

**Figure 6.1: Meakin and Dean's letter reluctantly agreeing to build the new Alnwick station, dated 27 August 1885, ending 'sooner than a stranger should come near us'.**

The contract for providing and fixing locking frames, signals, switch and signal connections was awarded to the Railway Signal Co., Liverpool, on 1 April 1886 for £4,874. A separate contract had been let to McKenzie and Holland, Worcester, for £1,600 on 4 June 1885 for the 12 sets of level crossing gates; the final cost came to £1,952. The actual cost of the signalling, excluding the gates, came to £9,797. The excess was made up of £1,328 for additional work on the original contract and the remainder for providing signalling and interlocking at places not included in the original invitation to tender.[7]

The motive power facilities received the same attention as everything else. The engine shed at Alnmouth was extended to accommodate the extra locomotives needed for the branch at a cost of £1,042. Cowans, Sheldon provided 50ft diameter turntables for installation at Alnwick and Coldstream for £325 each (plate 6.10); the cost of the foundations and siding was an extra £375 each.[8] There was a 'turntable siding' at Wooler, possibly in anticipation of the cattle train workings, but a turntable was never provided. Water for locomotive purposes was provided by means of a 2,000 gallons parachute column at Alnwick and by 7,500 gallons tanks at Whittingham and Wooler, each serving two columns (plate 6.17, fig. 6.9).

**Plate 6.10: the 50 feet diameter turntable and parachute water column provided at Alnwick in 1887 for working the branch. The start of the Alnwick & Cornhill is on the right of the picture. This is the only view in John Mallon's extensive collection of photographs showing cattle wagons on the line. In this case they are parked at the end of the branch probably waiting scrapping in the 1960s. P. B. Booth.**

In anticipation of the extra passengers at Coldstream a footbridge was authorised between the platforms for £370 and, later, extra waiting room accommodation costing £125.[9]

All the facilities provided seem to be based on the maxim 'if the job is worth doing it is worth doing well'. When the line was built it was expected that the railway would provide an essential service to the community for many decades, and that the safe and certain profits from the still expanding NER system would easily subsidise any losses made by the A&C and similar lines serving rural needs.

All the stations houses are now used as private dwellings. Many were conveyed during the 1960s 'in need of renovation' for very low prices. For example, in 1967 the station house, buildings and three cottages at Akeld were sold for £2,475, and a detached house and three cottages at Wooler for £1,200. Everything at Whittingham went for £5,250 in 1962.

Plate 6.11: the waiting shed on the up platform at Wooler painted in the chocolate (warm reddish-brown) and cream (pale yellow) colours used throughout the branch. This building was used as the men's accommodation for a YHA hostel from 1932 until the outbreak of World War 2. NERA 1887.

Plate 6.12: the 4-wagon warehouse at Whittingham was the same design as the one at Mindrum. The black building housed the platelayers' petrol driven trolley. J. F. Mallon c.1953.

Plate 6.13: the standard 2-wagon warehouse at Wooperton with a demonstration of riding a penny-farthing bicycle taking place c.1925. The one-ton hand crane can be seen to the right of the rider. J. F. Mallon collection.

Plate 6.14: although its population was very scattered, Mindrum's passenger figures show that nine journeys per head were made in 1901. As many of the passengers would come from Town Yetholm and Kirk Yetholm, some four miles away, this is a very creditable figure. This view looking north was probably taken in the 1950s. J. F. Mallon.

**Plate 6.15: Hedgeley 1887. NERA**

**Plate 6.16: Akeld looking west in the 1920s. J. Newbegin NERA.**

## ENDNOTES

1.  NER Traffic Committee (TC), 4 March 1886 and 29 April 1886.
2.  NER Way and Works (WW), 18 October 1883 and TC 16 September 1886.
3.  For full details of see Bill Fawcett's trilogy *A History of North Eastern Railway Architecture* published by the NERA between 2001 and 2005.
4.  PRO RAIL 527/646.
5.  WW 18 November 1886.
6.  WW 1 March 1888 and 19 April 1888.
7.  WW 17 November 1887.
8.  WW 8 and 22 September 1887. Drawings of the turntables and parachute water columns appear in *Servicing the North Eastern Railway's Locomotives* edited by John G. Teasdale (NERA 2007).
9.  TC 4 November 1886 and 6 October 1887.

52

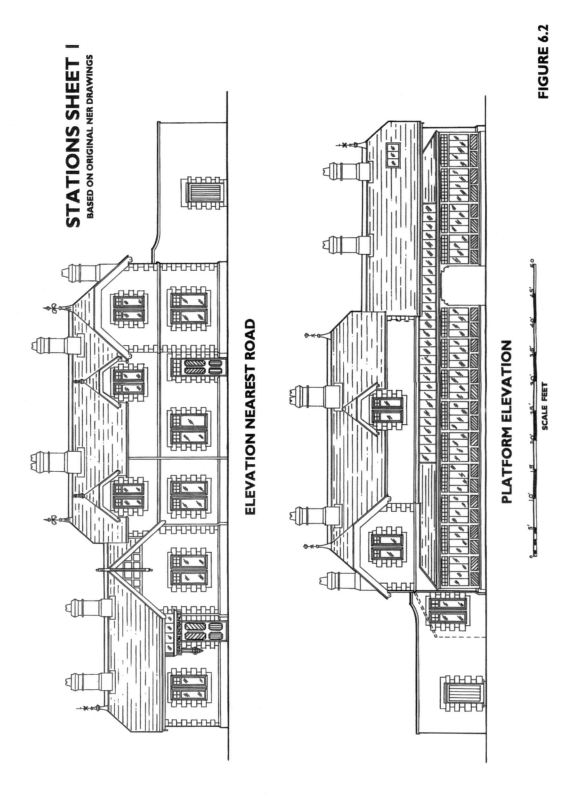

STATIONS SHEET I
BASED ON ORIGINAL NER DRAWINGS

ELEVATION NEAREST ROAD

PLATFORM ELEVATION

SCALE FEET

FIGURE 6.2

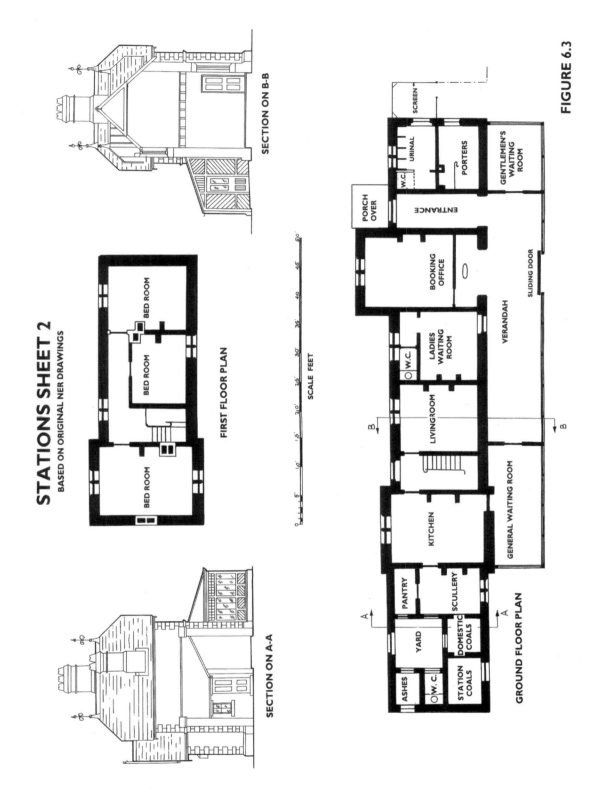

**STATIONS SHEET 2**
BASED ON ORIGINAL NER DRAWINGS

SECTION ON A-A

FIRST FLOOR PLAN

BED ROOM

BED ROOM

BED ROOM

SECTION ON B-B

SCALE FEET

GROUND FLOOR PLAN

ASHES

YARD

W. C.

PANTRY

DOMESTIC COALS

STATION COALS

SCULLERY

KITCHEN

GENERAL WAITING ROOM

LIVINGROOM

W.C.

LADIES WAITING ROOM

VERANDAH

SLIDING DOOR

BOOKING OFFICE

PORCH OVER

ENTRANCE

W.C.

URINAL

PORTERS

GENTLEMEN'S WAITING ROOM

SCREEN

**FIGURE 6.3**

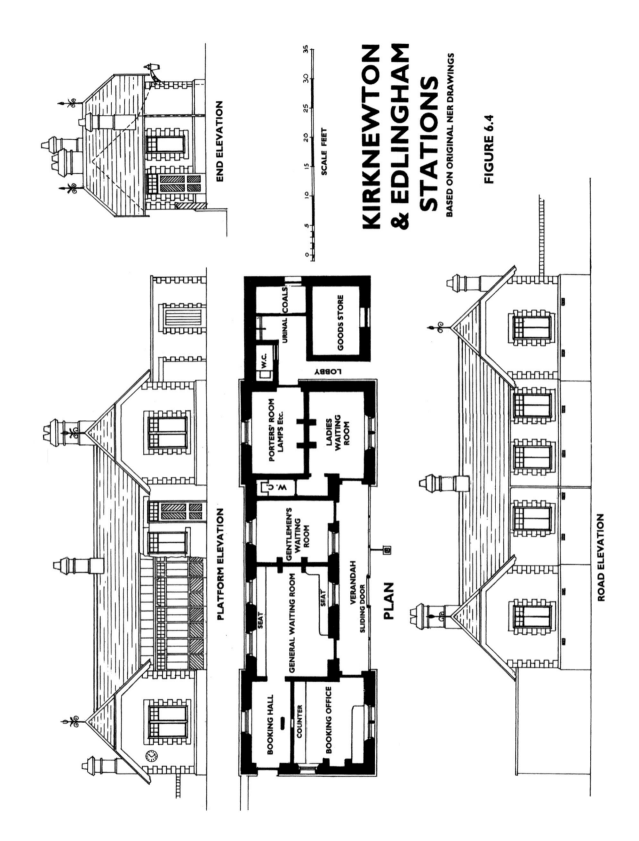

END ELEVATION

KIRKNEWTON
& EDLINGHAM
STATIONS

BASED ON ORIGINAL NER DRAWINGS

FIGURE 6.4

SCALE FEET

0  5  10  15  20  25  30  35

PLATFORM ELEVATION

PLAN

URINAL | COALS

GOODS STORE

W.C.

LOBBY

PORTERS' ROOM
LAMPS Etc.

LADIES
WAITING
ROOM

W.C.

GENTLEMEN'S
WAITING
ROOM

GENERAL WAITING ROOM

SEAT

SEAT

VERANDAH

SLIDING DOOR

BOOKING HALL

COUNTER

BOOKING OFFICE

ROAD ELEVATION

55

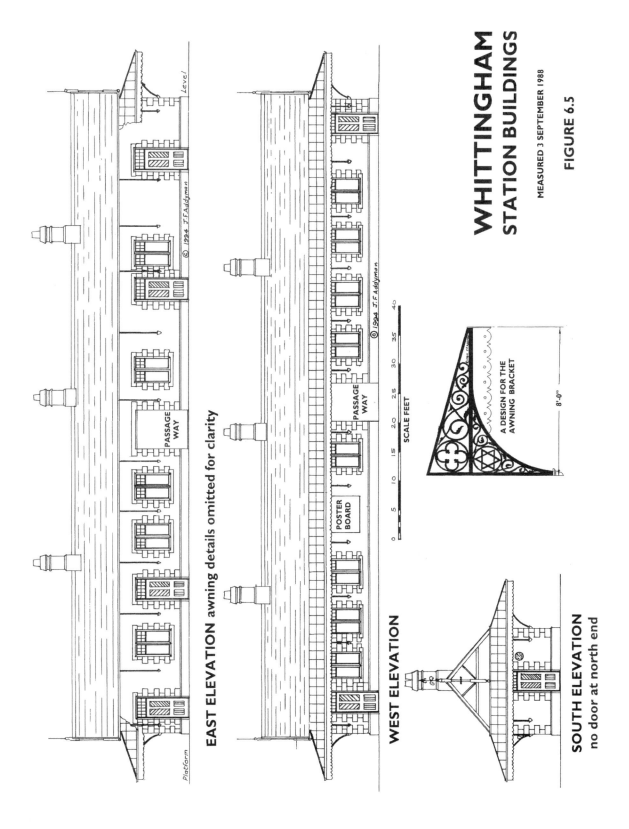

EAST ELEVATION awning details omitted for clarity

WEST ELEVATION

SOUTH ELEVATION
no door at north end

WHITTINGHAM
STATION BUILDINGS

MEASURED 3 SEPTEMBER 1988

FIGURE 6.5

A DESIGN FOR THE
AWNING BRACKET

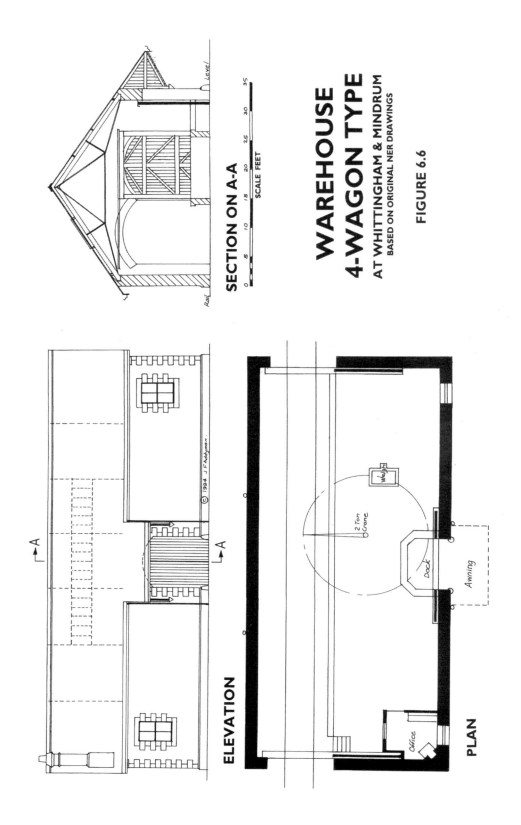

SECTION ON A-A

SCALE FEET
0  5  10  15  20  25  30  35

WAREHOUSE
4-WAGON TYPE
AT WHITTINGHAM & MINDRUM
BASED ON ORIGINAL NER DRAWINGS

FIGURE 6.6

ELEVATION

PLAN

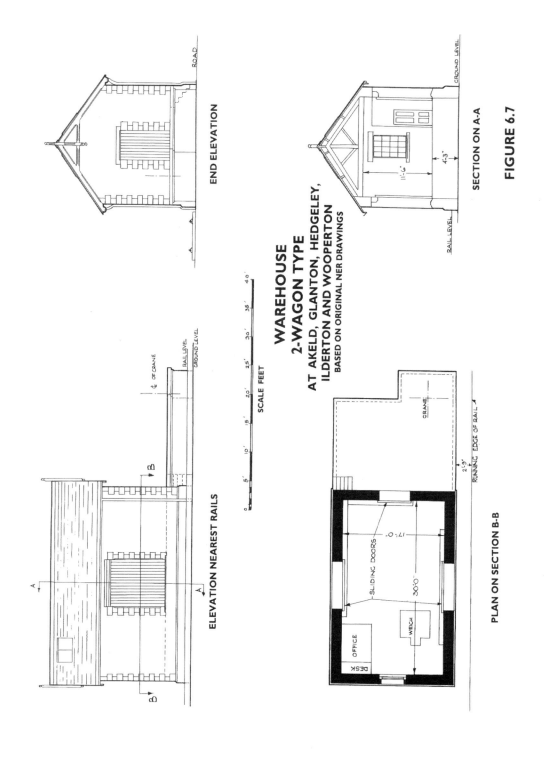

END ELEVATION

SECTION ON A-A

**FIGURE 6.7**

**WAREHOUSE
2-WAGON TYPE**
**AT AKELD, GLANTON, HEDGELEY,
ILDERTON AND WOOPERTON**
BASED ON ORIGINAL NER DRAWINGS

SCALE FEET

ELEVATION NEAREST RAILS

PLAN ON SECTION B-B

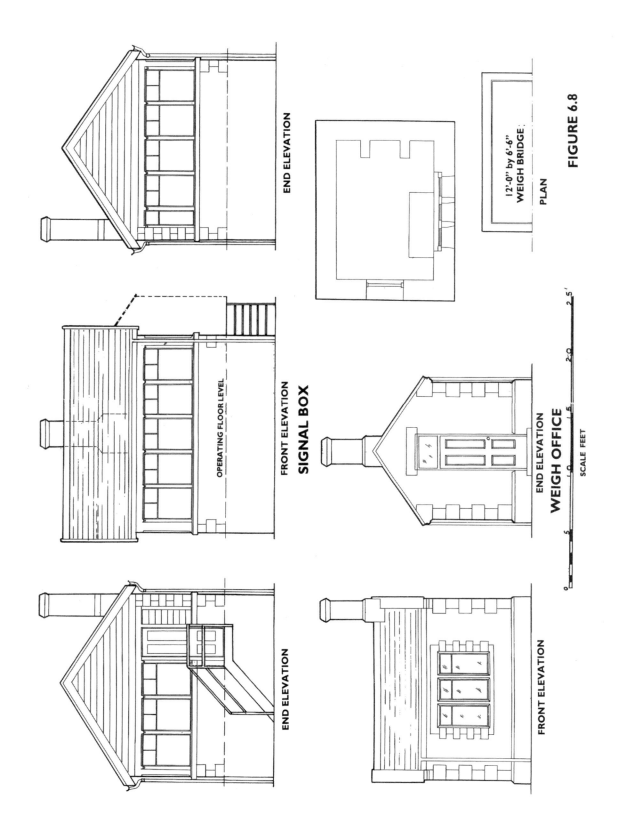

END ELEVATION

FRONT ELEVATION

**SIGNAL BOX**

END ELEVATION

OPERATING FLOOR LEVEL

END ELEVATION

**WEIGH OFFICE**

FRONT ELEVATION

12'-0" by 6'-6"
WEIGH BRIDGE

PLAN

SCALE FEET

**FIGURE 6.8**

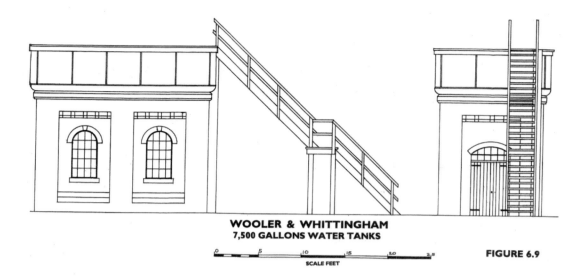

**WOOLER & WHITTINGHAM**
**7,500 GALLONS WATER TANKS**

SCALE FEET

**FIGURE 6.9**

**Plate 6.17: the water tank at Whittingham seen in a derelict condition in 1953. The DP plate at 25miles-70.87chains on the branch is the official point from which all the rates and fares for the station were worked out; it can be seen just to the left of the door. J. F. Mallon.**

CHAPTER SEVEN: PASSENGER SERVICES

Plate 7.1: the arrival of the first up train from Coldstream saw most of the population of Glendale assembled at Wooler station by 7-0am to witness the event. The number of people on the station footbridge must have severely tested the new structure. Crowds greeted the train all along the branch and some stationmasters put out bunting and flags to herald the event. Bogie Tank Passenger (BTP) class No. 199 heads an augmented rake of coaches for the occasion. NERA.

Plate 7.2: again most of the population of Alnwick seem to have turned out to see the first train from their new station to Coldstream. The official party led by Councillor Adam Robertson joined the 8-35am train here and returned on the evening train, which arrived 30 minutes late. Rain that had started in the late afternoon probably caused problems for the locomotive on the gradients approaching Summit. NERA.

During the feverish activity needed to get the line ready to pass the B.O.T inspection, staff had been taking up their appointments at the stations and signal boxes at the south end of the line. When dawn broke on 5 September 1887 many local residents contrived to be near the railway to witness an event which they had awaited for over 30 years. On this bright, sunny morning the first train left Coldstream at 6-38am hauled by a Fletcher BTP (Bogie Tank Passenger) 0-4-4T locomotive No. 199. The crimson painted rake of five 4-wheeled coaches, which had been specially built for use on the line, had arrived at Alnwick from the NER's workshops on the previous Thursday.

After being photographed at Wooler (plate 7.1) the train arrived at Alnwick at 8-18am. About 100 passengers joined the 8-35am to Coldstream, including an official party, which had booked a special carriage for the return journey from Alnwick (plate 7.2). Councillor Adam Robertson, who had done so much to get the railway built, was allowed the privilege of booking the first ticket for the branch at the impressive new station.[1] The party was made up of serving and retired members of the Local Board, some of their officials and members of the Press. They travelled to Coldstream, and then returned on the next train as far as Wooler, arriving in time to enjoy lunch at the Cottage Hotel. The lunch was followed by the self-congratulatory speeches usual at such events, but no gratitude was expressed to the NER or its shareholders for funding the line. One gentleman said; 'The railway was entirely due to the [Local] Board and its members'. However, there was a toast to the success of the railway.[2]

Prior to the railway opening the NER timetable advertised a coach service from the Star Hotel at Alnwick every day at 7-55 am; this returned from Wooler at 6-0 pm and arrived at Alnwick at 8-30 pm; this mail service had commenced in 1861. After the coming of the railway Lord's Day observance by the railway company meant that Sunday travellers were still dependent on coaches; one left the post office in Alnwick at 8-30 am and returned from Wooler at 6-0 pm. In the early years, omnibuses from the Star and Swan Hotels in Alnwick met almost every train from Coldstream and Alnmouth.

| STATION | POPULATION SERVED | TICKETS ISSUED 1901 |
|---|---|---|
| Wooler | 1,900 | 16,349 |
| Whittingham | 875 | 7,330 |
| Ilderton | 1,300 | 5,457 |
| Akeld | 420 | 5,518 |
| Hedgeley | 575 | 4,958 |
| Mindrum | 600 | 5,411 |
| Glanton | 740 | 4,861 |
| Wooperton | 500 | 3,229 |
| Kirknewton | 300 | 3,209 |
| Edlingham | 590 | 2,012 |
| TOTAL | 7,800 | 58,334 |

**Table 1: population served and tickets issued by the intermediate stations in 1901. The NER gave the total branch population, including Alnwick (8,000) and Coldstream (3,200), as 19,000. The stations are listed in order of their *total* receipts.**

Having made such a fuss to get their railway how did the locals support their passenger service? Because of the railway's novelty the last four months of 1887 generated more than average passenger bookings, but the journeys were shorter so the takings were no greater than in a normal four month period. The first excursion on the line left Wooler at 7-30am on Friday 24 September 1887 with 15 crowded coaches for the Newcastle Exhibition. However, the lack of regular excursions on the line was to be a bone of contention in its early years. It had been hoped that the railway would bring in large numbers of visitors, and increase the prosperity of the area (see Chapter 11).

The NER kept detailed statistics so it is possible to compare the branch's performance with the rest of the system. The population served by each station had been calculated from the census figures, taking in hamlets up to six miles from the railway. (Table 1) The industrial areas of Tyneside, Wearside and Teesside, with their commuter traffic, averaged between 10 and 14 journeys per head in 1910. By comparison in the same year the one-and-half millions served by the NER in the more rural Yorkshire did not quite equal the A&C's 1910 bookings of over six journeys per head. A point in favour of the branch was that the average fare, or length of journey, was more than double the figure for the whole NER system. As far as passenger figures were concerned the branch generated very reasonable revenue in relation to the sparse population it served, and the NER board would have been foolish to have expected anything better. If we think that some present-day rail fares are extortionate consider the 1890s when one hour's wage for a labourer would only buy four miles of rail travel; today's average can buy well over 50 miles. In 1890 a trip for a labourer and his family by rail was a luxury that would need careful budgeting.

The peak year for the branch was 1893 when a total of 62,500 tickets were booked at the intermediate stations, giving eight journeys per year per head of population. By 1922 the bookings had fallen to 43,500, giving under six journeys per head. This decline in passengers was not unique to the Alnwick and Coldstream as many other NER stations, without commuter or tourist traffic, showed a similar decline over the same period. Specimen figures suggest that 70% more tickets were collected at the stations on the branch than had been issued, but the majority of these would be from Alnwick or Coldstream with few of the remainder being from further afield than Newcastle or Berwick.

The first timetable gave a weekday passenger service of three trains a day in each direction. The journey time was a little over one-and-a-half hours, giving a very respectable average speed, including stops, of nearly 25 mph. (Such is progress that present day diesel railcars take the same time to cover the 35 miles from Middlesbrough to Whitby.) There was never a Sunday service on the branch; this resulted from a narrow-minded NER policy that denied many people excursions into the country on their only free day in the week.

**Table 2: the working timetable for the winter of 1892-3**

**26 I.**

### ALNWICK and COLDSTREAM—Weekdays.

| | | 1 | 2 | 3 | 4 | 5 | 6 | 8 | 9 | 10 | 12 | 14 | 16 |
|---|---|---|---|---|---|---|---|---|---|---|---|---|---|
| | | Empty Steam Autocar. | | PASSENGER. | | | **D** Goods. | **D** Goods. | | PASSENGER. | **D** Cattle. | STEAM AUTOCAR. | PASSENGER. |
| Distance from Alnwick. | DOWN. | MOQ | | | | | | | | | MOQ | | |
| | | dep. | | | | | arr. dep. | arr. dep. | | | arr. dep. | arr. dep. | arr. dep. |
| | | B a.m. | | a.m. | | | F a.m. a.m. p.m. p.m. | | | p.m. p.m. | B p.m. | H p.m. p.m. | p.m. p.m. |
| M. C. | **Alnwick** ‡ | — | | 8 35 | | | — 9 15 | — — | | 1 45 | — — | 5 17 | 7 10 |
| 4 26 | *Summit* ‡ | — | | .. | | | 9 35 9 40 | — — | | .. | — — | .. | .. |
| 7 0 | *Edlingham* ‡ | — | | 8 55 | | | 9 50 9 58 | — — | | 2 5 | — — | 5 36 | 7 30 |
| 9 70 | *Whittingham* ‡ | — | | 9 1 | | | 10 9 10 29 | — — | | 2 11 | — — | 5 42 | 7 36 7 37 |
| 11 47 | *Glanton* | — | | 9 6 | | | 10 36 10 50 | — — | | 2 16 | — — | 5 47 | 7 42 |
| 13 44 | *Hedgeley* ‡ | — | | 9 11 | | | 10°58 11 35 | — — | | 2 21 | — — | 5 52 | 7 47 |
| 15 57 | *Wooperton* ‡ | — | | 9 17 | | | 11 43 11 53 | — — | | 2 27 | — — | 5 58 | 7 53 |
| 18 49 | *Ilderton* ‡ | — | | 9 25 | | | 12 5 12 20 | — — | | 2 35 | — — | 6 6 | 8 1 |
| 22 13 | **Wooler** ‡ | 9 15 | | 9 33 | | | 12 32 — | — 12 50 | | 2 43 | — 3 30 | 6 12 6 16 | 8 10 |
| 24 63 | *Akeld* ‡ | .. | | 9 40 | | | — — | 1 0 1 10 | | 2 50 | 3 40 3 50 | 6 23 | 8 17 |
| 27 59 | *Kirknewton* ‡ | .... | | 9 47 | | | — — | 1 18 1 26 | | 2 57 | 3 58 4 5 | 6 30 6 47 | 8 25 |
| 30 8 | *Kilham Siding* | .. | | .. | | | — — | 1 34 1 39 | | .. | .. | .. | .. |
| 32 8 | *Mindrum* ‡ | .... | | 9 56 | | | — — | 1 46 2 5 | | 3 8 | 4 20 4 25 | 6 58 | 8 35 |
| 35 55 | **Coldstream** ‡ | 9 40 | | 10 3 | | | — — | 2 17 2 30 | | 3 17 | 4 35 | 7 5 7 8 | 8 44 8 45 |
| | Arrives at destination | Tweedmouth 10.5 a.m. p. 28 | | | | | | Tweedmouth 4.5 p.m. p. 28 | | | Tweedmouth 5.32 p.m. p. 28 | Berwick 7.33 p.m. p. 29 | Tweedmouth 9.13 p.m. p. 29 |

B—Runs on alternate Mondays, 6th and 20th July, 3rd, 17th, and 31st August, and 14th and 28th September when required.
F—Runs 5 minutes later Alnwick to Hedgeley on Mondays.

---

**I. 27**

### COLDSTREAM and ALNWICK—Weekdays.

| | | 1 | 2 | 3 | 4 | 7 | 8 | 10 | 12 | 14 | 17 | 21 | 24 |
|---|---|---|---|---|---|---|---|---|---|---|---|---|---|
| | | **D** Cattle. | PASSENGER. | **D** Goods and Cattle. | STEAM AUTOCAR. | **D** Goods. | PASSENGER. | **D** Cattle Empties. | **D** Goods. | **D** Goods. | **D** Goods. | STEAM AUTOCAR. | PASSENGER. |
| Distance from Coldstream. | UP. Departs from | Tweedmouth 4.50 a.m. p. 26 | Berwick 6.15 a.m. p. 26 | Kelso. 7.20 a.m. p. 28 | Tweedmo'th 8.0 a.m. p. 26 | | | Tweedmo'th 10.40 a.m. p. 26 | | | | Berwick 2.45 p.m. p. 27 | |
| | | MO | | MO | MO | | | MOQ | MO | M | MO | | |
| | | arr. dep. | | arr. dep. | | arr. dep. | | | arr. dep. | arr. dep. | arr. dep. | arr. dep. | arr. dep. |
| | | B a.m. a.m. | a.m. | E a.m. a.m. | EH a.m. | G a.m. a.m. | E a.m. | a.m. | p.m. p.m. | F p.m. p.m. | E p.m. p.m. | H p.m. dep. | p.m. p.m. |
| M. C. | **Coldstream** ‡ | 5 41 5 51 | 6 53 | 7 40 8 5 | 8 30 | — 10 | 5 10 40 | 11 20 | — — | — — | — — | 3 22 3 23 | 6 27 |
| 3 47 | *Mindrum* ‡ | 6 3 6 6 | 7 2 | 8°17 8 33 | 8 39 | 10°17 11 0 | 10 49 | .. | — — | — — | — — | 3 32 | 6 36 |
| 5 47 | *Kilham Siding* | .... | | 8 55 9 00 | .... | 11 7 11d12 | .... | | — — | — — | — — | .. | .. |
| 7 76 | *Kirknewton* ‡ | 6 20 6 25 | 7 11 | 9 5 9 15 | 9 5 | 11 20 11 28 | 10 58 | | — — | — — | — — | 3 41 | 6 45 |
| 10 72 | *Akeld* ‡ | 6 35 6 40 | 7 17 | 9 26 9 40 | 8 54 | 11 35 11 44 | 11 4 | .. | — — | 1 17 — | — 3 8 | 3 47 | 6 51 |
| 13 42 | **Wooler** ‡ | 6 50 7 0 | 7 25 | 9 43 — | 9 0 | 11 54 — | 11 13 | 12 0 | — — | — 1 17 | — — | 3 54 | 6 59 |
| 17 6 | *Ilderton* ‡ | 7 11 7 18 | 7 34 | — — | — — | — — | 11 22 | | 1 29 1 39 | 1 29 1 39 | 3 20 3 30 | 4 2 | 7 8 |
| 19 78 | *Wooperton* | 7 26 7 31 | 7 40 | — — | — — | — — | 11 26 | | 1 51 1 54 | 1 51 1 56 | 3 42 3 47 | 4 8 | 7 14 |
| 22 11 | *Hedgeley* ‡ | 7°38 7 55 | 7 45 | — — | — — | — — | 11 34 | | 1°4 2 4 | 2°4 2 32 | 3°55 4 43 | 4 13 | 7 20 |
| 24 8 | *Glanton* | 8 1 8 6 | 7 50 | — — | — — | — — | 11 39 | | 2 40 2 48 | 2 40 2 48 | 4 51 4 59 | 4 19 | 7 25 |
| 25 65 | *Whittingham* ‡ | 8 12 8 20 | 7 54 | — — | — — | — — | 11 43 | | 2 55 5 35 | 2 55 3 3 | 5 6 5 35 | 4 22 | 7 29 7 37 |
| 28 55 | *Edlingham* ‡ | 8°30 8 55 | 8 2 | — — | — — | — — | 11 51 | | 5 51 5 55 | 3 31 3 36 | 5 51 5 56 | 4 31 | 7 45 |
| 31 29 | *Summit* ‡ | 9 5 9 8 | .... | — — | — — | — — | — | | 6 3 6 13 | 3 48 3 53 | 6 8 6 13 | .. | .. |
| 35 55 | **Alnwick** ‡ | 9 20 9 45 | 8 22 | — — | — — | — — | 12 12 | | 6 25 — | 4 5 — | 6 25 — | 4 49 | 8 5 |

B—Morpeth arr. 10.35 a.m. p. 31.   E—Runs on alternate Mondays, 6th and 20th July, 3rd, 17th, and 31st August, and 14th and 28th September.   F—Runs on alternate Mondays, 13th and 27th July, 10th and 24th August, and 7th and 21st September.   G—Does not run on alternate Mondays, 6th and 20th July, 3rd, 17th, and 31st August, and 14th and 28th September.

**Tables 3&4; the summer 1908 working timetables.**

Within two months of the opening of the line the residents were again making demands, in a memorial to the NER board, requesting a market train from Coldstream to Alnwick on Saturday afternoons.[3] Initially, this application was refused by the Traffic Committee, but they relented and the train ran at least on Saturdays, and often more frequently, up to the end of World War 1. In February 1888 another memorial requested that the 8-35 am train from

Alnwick be timed an hour earlier to give a connection with the train from the south due at 7-27 am, and better connections from Coldstream to Edinburgh.[4] This request would have needed a total revision of the timetable and an additional train. The NER were not too worried about connections to the NBR for Edinburgh, but this application prompted them to look into connections to the NER midday trains to the south.

Coincidental with the opening of the line the new Wooler livestock mart was completed adjacent to the station, and additional passenger and cattle trains were timetabled to serve it. Sales were held on alternate Mondays throughout the year (after the end of WW1 this was changed to alternate Fridays). The basic timetable soon became established; the 1892-3 winter working timetable is given in Table 2.

The summer working timetable for 1908 is also reproduced in full (Tables 3 and 4), and shows the afternoon 'market trains' running daily as an autocar service (the NER's name for push-and-pull). In the winter they only ran on Mondays and Saturdays. Unlike 1939, when the onset of war brought an instantaneous curtailment of services, the start of the First World War had little or no immediate effect. The branch's services remained the same in 1915 as they had before the conflict. After the war the basic timetable of three passenger trains per day in each direction was worked until closure in 1930.

Soon after its opening, the NER had included the line on some of its holiday season promotions. It was featured in one of the 'Circular Tour Tickets' from Newcastle and Berwick, and was also included in four of the weekly or fortnightly 'Holiday Contract Tickets'. There is no indication that these significantly boosted the annual traffic figures.

**Plate 7.3: a rare picture of a passenger train on the line with class D17 (formerly M1) 4-4-0 No. 1625 at Birsley Wood near Edlingham c.1925. Two diagram 145 bogie coaches, built in 1910, were allocated to the branch and plated 'Aln'k & C'hill'. Miss Tait.**

After the peak of 1893 there had been a gradual but almost steady decline in the Alnwick & Cornhill's passengers until 1926, by which time the number of journeys had halved. The only improvement had been a transient increase in numbers immediately following the First World War. From 1926, following the introduction of local bus services, the railway's passengers almost disappeared. The buses had two great advantages over the trains: firstly, railway companies had to pay the total cost of maintaining their infrastructure, whereas the roads were maintained by the public purse, and secondly, railway stations were often remote from the villages that they served, but the buses could be routed through them.

It had been stated by the Select Committee, before the line was authorised, that the NER, as a large rich company, was under some obligation to cater for the more remote parts of its system. However, the NER directors, when accepting that the line would never be profitable, could not have possibly foreseen the major factors that were to affect all railways after 1914. The NER's gross revenue had almost doubled between 1880 and 1913, and, even with the significant rise in its operating costs during that period, it still paid a dividend of 7%. Under these circumstances some fall off in traffic on, already uneconomical, rural branch lines would have caused little concern.

The inflation during and after the 1914-1918 War meant that the cost of running the system was rising far more steeply than its revenue. The working expenses expressed as a percentage of the gross revenue (operating ratio) in 1922 were over 80% compared with 63% in 1913 and the 50% of the early 1880s. When the London & North Eastern Railway (LNER) took over in January 1923 the heavy industries in the North East had started the decline which would see them totally disappear over the next 60 to 70 years. The General Strike of 1926, the Wall Street crash of October 1929, and the severe recession that followed all added to the railway's problems. The upsurge of road transport, affecting both passengers and goods, was the last thing that the railways needed, and Parliament's shameful failure to give the railways the right to compete on an equal footing made the situation even worse.[5] None of these could have been anticipated by the NER directors, but their benevolence towards the social needs of people living in rural districts was to cost their successors dearly.

A typical report in the *Newcastle Journal,* in September 1930, stressed the serious and continuing decline of all traffic on the nation's railways: -

'The figures of the railway traffic receipts we publish this morning, which once again disclose heavy declines in gross income from both passenger and goods transport, call renewed attention to the difficult situation confronting the companies. Week after week, with monotonous regularity, decreases in the chief sources of income have been registered.'

'Competition from road transport has no doubt accounted for a considerable falling off in the railway companies' revenue from passenger traffic – the actual large number of people carried proving less remunerative – but the heaviest losses are shown in goods receipts, a corollary of the severe trade depression from which the country is suffering.'

The declining revenue prompted the LNER's North Eastern Area Board to look at possible savings on the A&C. Their first aim was to reduce the wages bill, and one way was by making economies at 11 of the level crossings on the branch (see Chapter 10). In another economy measure Edlingham became an unstaffed passenger halt only from 14 December 1925. However, goods handling was reinstated using 'public delivery siding facilities' from 23 August 1926; Whittingham was to deal with the paper work.[6] In 1922 the station master's salary at Edlingham was £200, but the revenue from all traffic was only £253-12s-1½d.

The measures described only produced relatively small savings, and something far more drastic had to be done about the A&C and other hopelessly uneconomic passenger lines. A special meeting of the LNER board, on 8 November 1928, 'considered the introduction of road services, which would enable the withdrawal, in certain circumstances, of existing passenger services.' As far back as 1903 the NER had started running a bus service between Beverley and North Frodingham, in the East Riding of Yorkshire. Though it had no specific powers to run the buses these were introduced in preference to building an authorised light railway.[7] The Railways Act of 1921 did not forbid the railways to operate road services, but in 1928 the LNER, together with the other main-line companies, consolidated their position and obtained formal powers under which they were able to purchase shares in road transport businesses. By 1931 the LNER had invested £2¼ million in road transport including the United Automobile Services, which operated throughout the North East.[8]

On 26 June 1930, the Divisional General Manager of the North Eastern Area presented a case to the LNER Traffic Committee for the withdrawal of passenger services on the Alnwick & Cornhill. He pointed out there had been a considerable decline in passenger traffic in recent years, due chiefly to road competition, and that the prospects of recouping the business were remote. He suggested discontinuing the branch service and taking off two of the trains that ran between Tweedmouth and Coldstream from September 1930. Parcels and miscellaneous passenger-rated traffic could be provided by re-arranging the branch goods train service, and running a parcels train in each direction. By these means the loss in parcels receipts was not expected to exceed £473. The savings in carriages were given as two brake composites with 16 first class and 90 third class seats, and in motive power one tank locomotive of class F8.

|  | Savings £ | Losses £ |
| --- | --- | --- |
| Permanent way maintenance | 1,225 |  |
| Locomotive power | 2,266 |  |
| Carriages | 127 |  |
| Traffic expenses | 2,571 |  |
| Cartage | 54 |  |
| **Total** | **6,243** |  |
| Passenger traffic |  | 1,805 |
| Parcels |  | 473 |
| **Total** |  | **2,278** |

**Table 5: showing savings of almost £4,000 following the withdrawal of passengers.**

The report concluded that: -

> 'There was a good road service by omnibus companies not associated with the LNER, and our associated company, United Automobile Services Ltd., are starting a service between Newcastle and Coldstream via Morpeth, Alnwick, Whittingham, Glanton and Wooler. Through services also ply between Newcastle and Edinburgh via Coldstream.'

The LNER board agreed that that the Alnwick and Cornhill, together with some other branches and intermediate stations, should lose their passenger services after Saturday 20 September 1930.[9] In all, 8% of the stations in the North Eastern Area lost their passenger services under similar economy measures between 1929 and 1931. (The LNER's Southern Scottish Area took a far less responsible view, and their, equally unremunerative, former NBR lines in Northumberland remained open for passengers into the 1950s)

The LNER made it clear that the stations affected would: -

> '...remain open for parcels, horse, milk and other perishable traffic, for which special parcel trains would be run. Passengers travelling by the company's associated bus services to join passenger trains at other stations would still be allowed to send their luggage in advance, and under the usual conditions, from or to any of the stations from which passenger services had been withdrawn.'

Before the end of August 1930, the LNER district passenger manager, in Newcastle, had informed the local councils about the impending closure of the line. The Glendale Council, based in Wooler, expressed concern that the substitute bus service would go direct from Wooler to Cornhill (via the A697), and that Kirknewton and Mindrum would be without a service. One councillor (was he an LNER shareholder?) agreed that 'the railway company could not be expected to run trains when nobody travelled on them.' Others suggested that the use of the LNER's recently introduced steam railcars would allow the railway to compete with the bus fares.

The LNER replied: -

> 'Whilst the times of the proposed road service are not definite, it was intended that these will serve the whole of the stations on the branch with the exception of Edlingham, Mindrum and Kirknewton. I am taking up the question with the United Company to see whether or not they are prepared to introduce a service from these places. A connection will be made at Alnwick with trains to and from the Newcastle direction.

'With regard to the point you raised about the fares, I would remind you that the Railway Company, on October 22$^{nd}$ 1928, introduced experimental fare tickets at considerable reductions to the ordinary fares, and these were practically on a level with those of the motor bus companies [almost all the tickets sold in 1930 had been at the 'experimental rates']. Despite this we were not successful in getting back the traffic to any extent.' [10]

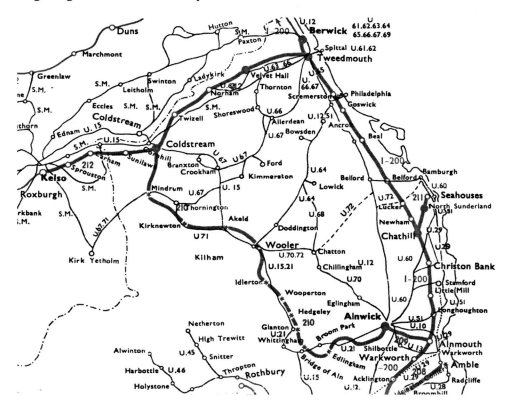

**Figure 7.1: a map showing the bus services operating in the area by the mid-1930s. The 'U' prefix denotes United services, and 'SM' Scottish Motor Traction Co. Ltd.**

Soon, bus services were provided to all the villages by the United Automobile Services Ltd. and the Scottish Motor Traction Co. Ltd. (jointly owned by the LNER and LMS). The map above shows the routes that were covered, although some would only represent a limited service on market days. Eventually, the buses encountered the same problems as the railways had, and lost out to the motor car. They were gradually withdrawn leaving many hamlets as badly off, for public transport, as they had been 150 years ago.

The *Newcastle Journal* reported on the final journey of the 6-42pm train from Alnwick to Coldstream, which departed on 20 September to the sound of exploding detonators with 60 people on board, and commented: -

'There was something tragically pathetic about the way in which the Alnwick and Cornhill Railway, in picturesque North Northumberland, virtually passed out of existence at the weekend, so far as the travelling public is concerned.'

'It was an open secret for many years past, this particular branch had not been an economic proposition. In the old days, before the advent of the all-conquering motor, the Railway Company could rely on a fair number of passengers. Indeed during the holiday season and on special occasions such as the Wooler show day and Alnwick hirings, it often took the authorities all their time to cope with the heavy volume of traffic.'

'Things have changed now. For one thing many former travellers – for the most part farmers domiciled maybe a matter of miles from the nearest railway station – now have their own motors. Added to this, of later years the railways have had to face a new and even more powerful rival in the shape of the ubiquitous motor-bus.'

'In the face of such fierce competition traffic receipts have dropped steadily – so much so that the Railway Company has become tired of running trains in which scarcely anyone has shown a wish to travel, and has accordingly now closed the line to passenger traffic. This, to say the least, is a great pity, for the railway cost a little mint of money to build, and it is inconceivable that the Company can have anything like recovered themselves [their outlay].'

The reporter alighted at Wooler and interviewed the stationmaster, Mr. Bainbridge, who was due to retire at the end of the month after almost 50 year's service. Oddly, he blamed the 1926 General Strike, and not the buses, for the decline on the railway: -

'When I came here six years ago we had a fair volume of passenger traffic. In the holiday season indeed, I have seen the platforms simply black with would be travellers. Latterly, the nearest we have had to a crowd has been on the agricultural show days. Even then, we did not get a big crowd this last time.'

Fred Hollamby, son of Wooperton's first stationmaster, succeeded Mr. Bainbridge at Wooler, and he, in turn, was followed by Arthur Bird, son of Ilderton's first stationmaster.

**Plate 7.4: the last passenger train to Alnwick passing Summit on 20 September 1930 hauled by class D17 (formerly M1) No. 1625. M. Halbert.**

Another link back to the beginning was John Hinson, who had worked for the contractors building the line, and had then been given the position of a passenger porter at its opening. He had been a signalman at Wooler for the last 36 years and, as such, had signalled the last regular passenger train through. The closure meant that he would have to be reduced to a porter/signalman if he wanted to remain at Wooler. Only a few staff on the branch would be displaced, and work would be available for them on other parts of the LNER system.

Under the new arrangements, the early morning train was replaced by a van which delivered newspapers and mail between Alnwick and Wooler, and the evening train by a bus which departed from Alnwick station forecourt at 5-35pm, taking any passengers who had arrived from Newcastle. The afternoon train was replaced by the parcels train leaving

Alnwick about 2-00pm, and returning from Coldstream at about 4-30pm. The goods service remained the same, with cattle and sheep specials when necessary.

Parcels traffic, which was counted as passenger revenue, had increased dramatically on the NER system from the 1880s. The new Alnwick station had a large parcels office built into it, and in 1921 it handled over 50,000 parcels. Appendix 3 gives typical charges for parcels. The total for all the intermediate stations on the branch, in the same year, was 44,000. Milk in cans, fish, horses, dogs, bicycles, cars or carriages and game all counted as 'Passenger Items'. Hedgeley, for example, forwarded around 15 tons of game per annum, and Glanton over 1,800 12 gallon milk cans. Wooler and Kirknewton both dispatched over 30 tons of fish in 1922, (the Bowmont Water was considered one of the best trout streams in the North East, but 25 to 30 thousand fish seems a remarkable number).[11] The gentry used the railway to take horses to hunts or race meetings; a famous horse being *Jazz Band,* owned by Mr. Adam Scott of Alnham (served by Whittingham), which won the Northumberland Plate, at Newcastle, in 1923. Less valuable horses could be sent as livestock traffic.

At many of the branch's intermediate stations, by the 1920s, the revenue from the 'passenger items' equalled or exceeded that obtained from ticket sales. Although parcels traffic was now heading towards a loss over the whole system, the LNER considered it worthwhile to run a parcels train to retain this traffic after the withdrawal of the passenger service. It was this parcels train that was to provide a very limited passenger service, from 1934, to give access to the railway's holiday accommodation. There were also some scenic excursions during the summers of the 1930s.

**Figure 7.2: Extract from a 1938 LNER map showing YHA hostels (circles) and the railway holiday accommodation (squares)**

In July 1933 the LNER started introducing camping coaches, and by 1938 there were 55 locations in the North Eastern Area where holiday accommodation was available in coaches or railway premises.[12] On the Alnwick & Cornhill there was a mixture of accommodation provided in railway cottages or station buildings, as well as in coaches. After the number of railway staff had been reduced some cottages were permanently let to local tenants, but some remained vacant and were made available for holiday-makers. Kirknewton lost its stationmaster in December 1927 and Akeld in December 1932; from 1935 the station premises at both were let as holiday apartments.[13] Accommodation was advertised on the branch in 1938 at all the stations except Wooler and Edlingham. Parts of Wooler station had been used as a Youth Hostel Association hostel from 1932,[14] and Edlingham only featured in the 1933 listings after which its location was considered too remote. A condition for using the railway accommodation was that the holiday makers must arrive by train or by 'a mode of conveyance' approved by the passenger manager at York. This was achieved on the branch by re-introducing a 'passenger service' by attaching a coach to the Saturday parcels trains.

In the panic immediately at the outbreak of war, in September 1939, large numbers of evacuees started arriving from Tyneside to Wooler by rail. The first to arrive were 280 pupils and teachers from North View School, Heaton, 'punctual to schedule'. The next day 110 mothers and infants arrived, and the following week, 317 children and teachers arrived from Tynemouth. This vast number of evacuees was distributed around households in the town and in the villages of Ingram, Roddam, Lilburn, Crookham, Ford, Branxton, Kirknewton, Doddington, Fenton, Chatton, Mindrum, Milfield, Lowick and Bowsden. The schools took over some large country houses.[15]

During the war, Akeld gained importance as the railhead for the new RAF airfield at Milfield, and its booking office was again manned. Troop trains arrived from the south, and tickets were issued for the weekend leave trains to Tweedmouth. In 1942 there were 1,404 tickets booked and 558 collected, which together with the parcels, fish and fruit handled gave a total passenger revenue of £3,103. However, the figures for 1943 show only 65 tickets booked and 370 collected, with total takings of just £680.[16] The leave trains used 'old coaches without lights, and sometimes without windows', so it is not surprising if the buses to

Coldstream or Berwick soon won most of the traffic.[17] Both during and after the war, rabbits formed a large part of the line's parcels traffic, as the 40 rabbit catchers employed by the Northumberland War Agricultural Committee caught thousands of pairs weekly. The rabbits were in great demand in the towns to supplement the meagre meat rations.

In May 1942 Glendale Council's application to the LNER for a daily passenger service using two coaches attached to the parcels train was refused. They decided to take their plea to 'higher authority' and got the backing of Berwick M.P., Captain Grey, who took it up with the Minister of Transport. Although petitions had been raised in the villages near every station the Ministry announced, in December, that it would be impossible reopen the passenger service, and stated that 'engines and railway staff were now working at high pressure.'[18]

In 1946 Akeld booked 11 journeys with total passenger traffic receipts of £595, but the following year saw two passengers and receipts down to £110. There was a final rail tour from Coldstream to Wooler in April 1963 hauled by an ex LMS mogul No. 46474. With parcels and goods traffic almost gone, how much longer could the line remain open? (See Chapter 9).

## ENDNOTES

1. The contract for glazing and painting the new station had been awarded to Adam Robertson & Co.
2. *Alnwick & County Gazette* (*AG*) 10 September 1887.
3. Traffic Committee 3 November 1887.
4. Ibid. 1 March 1888.
5. E. A. Gibbins, *Square Deal* (1998) gives an explanation of the railways' problems.
6. General Manager's Circular 5/1926. DGM Leeds' Circular No. 172 31 August 1926.
7. Ken. Hoole, *NER Buses, Lorries and Autocars* (1969) p.12.
8. G. Hughes, *LNER* (1986) p. 126.
9. PRO RAIL 390/61.
10. *AG* 26 September 1930.
11. NER Traffic Returns.
12. LNER Map 1938.
13. A. McRae, *British Railway Camping Coach Holidays Parts 1 & 2* (1997).
14. Sir Charles Trevelyan formally opened the Youth Hostel on 18 June 1932. Men were accommodated in the up side waiting room, and women in the verandah on the opposite side; the station toilets were used as wash rooms. The hostel closed at the start of the war.
15. *AG* 8 September 1939.
16. Annual reports for Akeld Station.
17. Letter from F. Stainforth , who served at RAF Milfield, to John Mallon.
18. *AG* 22 May 1942.

**Plate 7.5: Porter/signalman W. Laycock and his wife with holidaymakers from the 'camping cottage' at Akeld in the summer of 1948. J. Mallon.**

## SIDING DIAGRAMS

The siding layouts for the stations are taken from the original NER siding diagrams. Wooler appears as figure 3.3.

### EDLINGHAM 1919

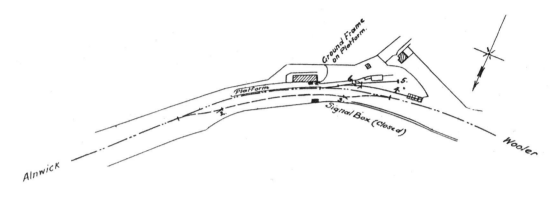

### WHITTINGHAM 1918

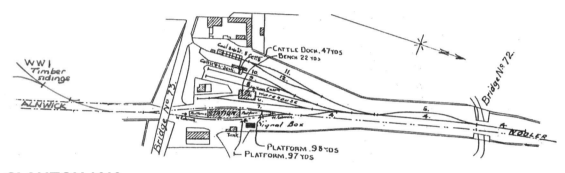

### GLANTON 1918

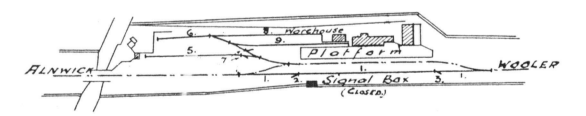

### HEDGELEY 1919

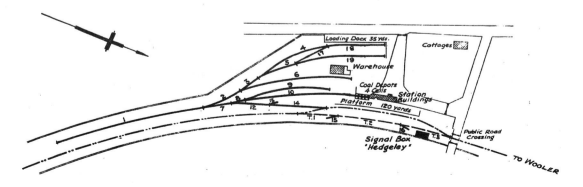

## WOOPERTON 1924

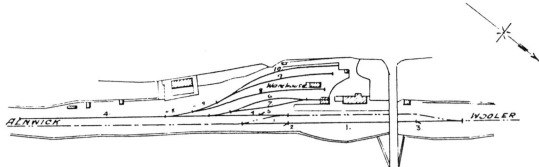

## ILDERTON 1916

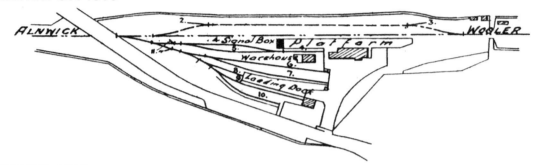

## AKELD 1918

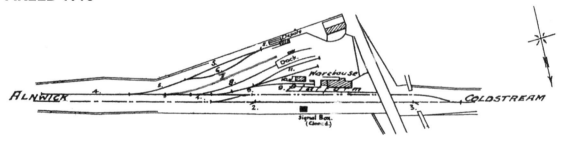

## KIRKNEWTON AND KILHAM SIDINGS 1918

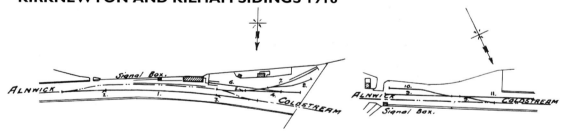

## MINDRUM 1919

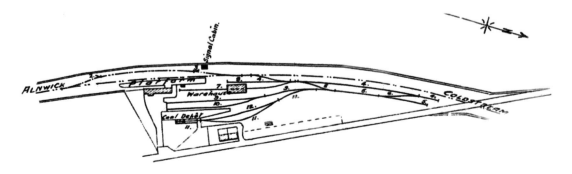

## CHAPTER EIGHT: STAFF AND PASSENGERS

### The Staff

At the beginning of May 1887 it was reported that 'a special train left Newcastle conveying stationmasters, porters, signalmen, clerks and others with their wives and families to the places allotted to them on the new line.' The goods service, of one train a day in each direction, started between Coldstream and Wooperton on 9 May. The stationmasters and staff at Hedgeley, Glanton, Whittingham and Edlingham were not appointed until September, when the branch was fully opened. Originally, the stationmasters were paid £1 per week except at Whittingham and Wooler, where it was 5 and 10 shillings more[1]. Their accommodation was free until after the First World War when rents were deducted from their, by then, much larger salaries. Their income was supplemented by as much as 50% from acting as agents for the sale of coal from the station yard, which the NER encouraged. At one time, the Post Offices at Wooperton and Mindrum were in the station office with the stationmasters acted as sub-postmasters. The names of the first stationmasters are given in Appendix 4.

Some of the stationmasters remained in their posts for the rest of their lives. William Bird, the first stationmaster at Ilderton died there in 1925. Before his appointment, in April 1887, he had been a senior clerk at Alnwick. On 2 September 1902, he had been involved in a terrible tragedy; his 11 month old son had crawled out into the station yard, and was run over by a cart collecting coal before he could rescue him.

From 1889 the NER started to offer £2 and £1 as first and second class prizes for 'best displays of plants and shrubs' in station gardens. The stationmasters at the smaller stations were only earning £1 per week so the prizes were quite generous, and did generate fierce competition. In 1895 the NER system was divided into four sections with 15 prizes allotted to each section: -

| Total Prizes | To the Station-master | To the Staff |
|---|---|---|
| 5 of £6 each | £4 | £2 |
| 5 of £3 each | £2 | £1 |
| 5 of 30s each | £1 | 10s |

In 1907 the prizes ranged from £10 for 'special class' to £2 for 'third class' with an additional award of £5 for a 'beginners' class': 'the division of the money to the staff concerned being left to the discretion of the stationmaster'.[2]

Henry Hollamby, who served almost 30 years at Wooperton before his death on 30 December 1916, was famous for his gardens, winning 1st class prize in 1911 and 2nd class in 1913 (plates 8.1 and 8.2). Photographs of the station appeared in the *NER Magazine* in 1911, 1914 and 1915. His obituary recorded: 'Wooperton station was made quite famous by Station Master Hollamby for its floral decorations. He was a pioneer of railway station flower gardens, which later received deserved encouragement by the introduction of competition between stations of the North-Eastern Railway Company, with prizes awarded yearly.' Mrs. F. L. Mather, of Newcastle, wrote to the NER in 1911, recalling Wooperton in 1887 as 'a howling wilderness devoid even of soil – nothing but sand on which no plant would grow. Slowly and laboriously the stationmaster and his staff brought soil from adjoining hedge and roadsides, and now blossoms like a rose what was once nothing but a desert.' [3]

All the stationmasters took a pride in their work, (Wooler won a prize in 1913) and the gardens gave a lot of pleasure to travellers, typically: -

> 'Hedgeley station on the west line is very pretty just now, in a wealth of floral colour. There is a profusion of roses, some of these being lovely. The sweet peas however, attract most eyes. The plants are tall, the tendrils as high as one's head and they are nearly in full bloom. Some of the flowers are very big, and some

four or five on a stalk. I congratulate Mr. Clayton, the stationmaster on his early and splendid show.' [4]

**Plate 8.1: Stationmaster Hollamby with his display of flowers inside the verandah at Wooperton station c. 1912. J. F. Mallon collection.**

**Plate 8.2: part of the display on Wooperton station platform. J. F. Mallon collection.**

In 1925 Edlingham, Glanton and Ilderton lost their stationmasters, with Kirknewton following in 1927. Initially, Edlingham was controlled by Whittingham, Glanton by

Hedgeley, Ilderton by Wooperton and Kirknewton by Akeld. In November 1930 Ilderton and Wooperton came under Wooler's control, and Akeld followed in December 1932. Mindrum was controlled by Coldstream from June 1931. Hedgeley and Wooler had stationmasters until the final closure of their sections, but Whittingham's was appointed to Christon Bank a year before the south end of the line was closed.[5]

The signalmen, porters and platelayers lived in the cottages provided for them along the line (plate 8.3). At most of these water had to be pumped from a well, and, of course, oil lighting was all that was available. At Wooler, an offer by the local gas company to supply the railway premises was turned down by the NER in 1885.[6] Some remote cottages had their water delivered by the goods trains. The NER ran a stores train which supplied all its branches with everything from oil for the signals to stationery for stations. It served each branch on a monthly basis, and the dates were published in the current Working Timetable.

**Plate 8.3: Wooler South with the detached cottage conveniently provided for the signalman. The railway company had to contribute £100 towards the cost of the bridge in the foreground (see page 27). Photo c.1900 from the J. F. Mallon collection.**

The maintenance of 'Way and Works' came to one-sixth of the NER's total expenditure, but nothing is ever written about the thousands of platelayers, whose work was so essential to the safe running of the trains. They don't get mentioned because they carried out their work with quiet efficiency, and rarely caused problems. Many on the A&C must have started work as agricultural labourers, who, tired of the uncertainty and indignity of the Annual Hirings, preferred a steady, and at least as well paid, job on the railway. When the maintenance of the A&C was taken over by the district engineer from the contractor's men, on 30 November 1887, the line had been divided into gangers' lengths under the control of the permanent way inspector at Wooler. Each gang, of three to five men, was responsible for about three miles of track. The work was governed to some extent by the seasons as it was obviously better, or even essential, to perform some tasks at certain periods of the year. For example, ballast riddling, packing and aligning of the track should never be carried out in very hot weather for fear of buckling the track, and controlling lineside growth was a job for early spring.

All railways have an obligation to maintain fencing to keep livestock off the line, and it was up to the platelayers to see that this was done. The fence posts were always on the railway side to prevent large animals from dislodging the rails, but if fence rails got broken, and animals were killed by a train, the railway had to pay compensation. When 10 sheep were killed near Akeld, on 16 February 1895, the railway was faced with a claim of £40; the engineer, Charles Harrison, was delegated to settle 'on the best terms'.[7]

After the withdrawal of the passenger service the maintenance standards, and, therefore, manning levels could be reduced to produce annual savings of £1,225. As on a number of other lightly used LNER branches, the A&C became maintained by bigger gangs covering a much greater length. These used petrol driven rail motors (often referred to as 'pneumonia bogies'), working under special signalling instructions, to get them about (plate 8.4).

**Plate 8.4: J. Tait and J. Athey on one of the petrol driven trolleys used on the branch to allow a reduced number of platelayers to cover a much larger area. J. F. Mallon**

The locomotives and their crews are much better reported, and a number of incidents are given in Chapter 11. The first member of the NER staff to drive on the line was probably Robert Young, a fireman from Alnmouth shed. He was loaned to the contractors in July 1886 to drive *Sambo*, which had earlier been involved in a derailment and a fire near the line caused by sparks from its chimney.

At the end of December 1891 an Alnmouth driver, John Carter, was killed in a shunting accident at Whittingham. During the shunting operations he had left two wagons very close to the fouling point on a siding. According to the porter's evidence at the inquest: 'there was only room for the engine to pass the wagons, but not for a man to put his head many inches from the engine.' Thomas Dinning, the fireman stated: -

> 'Before they got to the wagons, the deceased shut off steam and looked out. He (the witness) then heard a crash and looking round saw he had got his head fast between the engine and the first wagon. He at once stopped the engine, reversed the steam, and ran it clear of the wagons. The deceased seemed to have been killed instantly.'[8]

The jury returned a verdict of 'accidentally killed while in the execution of his duty.'

One of the early regular drivers on the line was Elijah Hodgson, who had fired class M1 4-4-0 No. 1621 during the 1895 'Races to the North' (London to Aberdeen). He became a driver of class N10 0-6-2T No. 1667, and later of the famous No. 1621, when it became allocated to Alnmouth towards the end of its life. No. 1621, now as LNER class D17/1, made its last revenue-earning trip on the A&C in July 1945, when part of its reversing gear broke on the descent from Summit to Alnwick. It was immediately withdrawn for preservation, and is now exhibited at the National Railway Museum, York. According to Jack Forsyth, he and other Alnmouth drivers had found No. 1621 one of their best engines to work as 'she was easy to fire and very responsive'. She may have been fine on semi-fast passenger trains to Newcastle or Tweedmouth, but one questions if 7ft. 1¼in. diameter driving wheels were ideal for the long 1 in 50 gradients on the branch. The classes of locomotives known to have run on the line are given in Appendix 5.

Most of the wagons used on the line were without continuous brakes that could be controlled by the locomotive. It was standard practice, before descending steep gradients, to pin down the brakes on a sufficient number of wagons to enable the engine and guard's van to control the train. One driver had not pinned down enough, and found the brakes were not responding. He ended up, somewhat shaken, just short of the buffer stop in one of the sidings at Alnwick station.

As the goods and parcel's service did not have to run to a strict timetable, the train could be stopped for members of the crew to go mushrooming or catching rabbits with ferrets. One of the guards, 'Jack' Hopper, who did a considerable amount of poaching on the line, sometimes had problems. On one poaching expedition he fell into the Bowmont Water, and had to carry out his duties all the way back to Alnwick wearing only his railway raincoat and boots. Another time he got left behind at Whittingham, and had to walk back to Alnwick. The driver had intended to take water at the station, which should have allowed time to catch the odd rabbit, but as the tank was half-full the driver decided to proceed, unwittingly leaving his guard behind. He was offered a lift in a car to take him to Edlingham to catch up with the train, but refused as he considered he would be in more trouble if he left railway premises than if he walked back to Alnwick along the track.[9] A former fireman, who wished to remain nameless, told of how on arrival at Whittingham, the crew would proceed to the nearby Bridge of Aln pub where their pints were ready for them on the bar. An easy life when compared with firemen on other parts of the system who often had to shovel over one-and-a-half tons of coal in an hour.

**The Passengers**
Some of the passengers on the very first train from Alnwick, Messrs, Worsdell and Raven from the NER locomotive department, E. B. Forbes, the resident engineer, and J. Simpkin, a senior permanent way inspector from Newcastle, would not have had any fears about the journey. However, other passengers were a little worried when the train started to accelerate rapidly down the 1 in 50 gradient, after passing Summit, 'the rugged exterior of rock on either side appeared to fly past at almost lightning speed… We were soon convinced that there was nothing to fear, as the train ran almost as smoothly along the rails as we had been used to on the main line. After gracefully taking the curves at what may be termed the bottom of the steepest part of the gradient, we were ushered into Edlingham station...'

A wagonette was available to take passengers between Glanton village and the railway (1 mile), and two of the earliest passengers were Dr. Robertson and his daughter Elizabeth. She felt that the train 'certainly is a great improvement on the old system of driving across the Moor, especially in the winter months. Papa was a little nervous on the return journey. We did come down to Edlingham at a reeling pace.' The drivers obviously knew how fast they could go as there is no record of a mishap due to excessive speed.

The railway made it possible for the wealthier people in the country to visit the towns to shop or see friends, but for some of them it involved a lengthy walk to the station if transport was not available. Local businessmen and traders made good use of the line, and travelling salesmen, laden with suitcases, went out to the villages to sell to customers in their own homes. Apparently, women of the Salvation Army were a familiar sight in the villages going from door-to-door selling all manner of beautiful handmade garments.

W. Dixon, who ran the general dealer's shop in Glanton, travelled by rail to Newcastle to obtain items that his customers had ordered, and these duly arrived by train. The shop stocked a wide range of goods including, groceries, ready-made clothing, hats, footwear, household china, linens, furniture and fittings, hardware and stationery. In 1889 Glanton was doing well by providing accommodation for rail-borne visitors in 11 private houses and at the two inns.

Others considered that: -

> '...easier transport by the railway was to prove a mixed blessing for Glanton and other villages. It was no longer essential for the gentry to keep their horses and carriages which meant less work for men. Even if villagers did not flock to the towns to make their normal purchases, the rapid increases in cheapness and availability of manufactured goods was a new factor in the situation for village craftsmen and village shops.'

Postmen boarded the morning train at Alnwick, alighting at various stations to walk their 'round' of many miles before returning by the evening train. From 1891, Robert Rutherford travelled to Ilderton station to begin his deliveries to West Lilburn, Lilburn Grange, Newtown, Hepburn Bell, Quarry House, and finally Chillingham. He reached Chillingham Castle at mid-day, and met up with a postman, who had covered another round, to have lunch with the maids in the kitchen. After a rest and a gossip the men returned over their rounds to collect letters, as it was customary for country folk to place letters prominently in their windows for the postmen to see. The distance walked each day was about 12 miles.[10]

**Plate 8.5: two postmen (Mr. Tiffin centre) having completed their rounds await the train back to Alnwick from Glanton. J. F. Mallon collection**

Major A. H. Browne was the owner of Callaly Castle, about three-and-a-half miles from Whittingham station. One of the early excursions on the branch took place in 1891, when a large party of members of the Newcastle Society of Antiquaries made a visit to the castle to view Major Browne's collection of ancient Greek vases, 'one of the fullest, and most valuable, to be found in any existing museum'. A special train ran between Alnwick and Whittingham to connect with the main-line services.

When the Browne's wanted to travel, their son, Alec (born in the late 1890s), recalled in his '*Recollections of a Small Boy*' that they did so in style. When they visited his grandfather in Cornwall in summer they travelled in a saloon 'a thing like a dining-car' with third-class compartments at each end. The compartments housed his mother's maid, his father's valet, a footman, his nurse and nursery maid. The saloon took them from Whittingham and arrived at King's Cross in the evening, where the family stayed at the Great Northern Hotel. Next morning they rejoined the saloon which had been attached to the Cornish train at Paddington.

When Alec was a little older, he was sent to a preparatory school in the South. The long journey meant that when he returned at holiday times he had missed the last train to get to Whittingham from Newcastle: -

'Well, in those days, one could get a special train for three (I think it was) first-class tickets. So three first-class tickets were produced for me, and I used to go in a special train. There were two fellows on the engine, the driver and stoker, the guard and me. We duly arrived at Whittingham station where I was met by a Brougham and taken up to Callaly.'

In comparison, a labourer in those days would use nearly one-tenth of his weekly wage just on a third-class return trip from Whittingham to Alnwick.

Schoolchildren attending the Duke and Duchess' Grammar Schools in Alnwick, travelled by train from as far afield as Wooler. The boys and girls were required to occupy separate carriages, and both objected to adult intruders. The girls had a problem with 'a little gentleman in a bowler hat' who seemed to enjoy their company. On one occasion, after he dozed off, the girls shouted the name of his intended station, whereupon he jumped out just as the train was about to leave, not realising until too late that he was one station short of his destination! The boys were annoyed by a lady who persisted in travelling in their compartment, and one decided to play a trick on her. When the train entered the darkness of Hillhead Tunnel, he opened the compartment door and quickly slammed it shut. He then hid under the seat, and when the train emerged from the tunnel his absence was noted with great alarm by the lady, who reported it to the stationmaster at Whittingham. While she was on the platform, the lad alighted on the track side, out of sight of those on the platform, and went home. Whether he ever admitted what he had done to his father, who was the Whittingham stationmaster, is not recorded.

When the train was struggling up to Summit the boys would jump out and walk alongside it, then clamber back in before it started to pick up speed on the down gradient. One youngster recalled travelling after dark in, 'steamy gas-lit compartments – they had a mouldy gas smell all of their own.'

In the bad winter of 1947 two older students travelled from Edinburgh to Wooler for a weekend, against the advice of their college. Because of the worsening weather the girls could not get back to Berwick via Cornhill or Belford, but the railway was open to Alnwick and the friendly stationmaster suggested they could travel as 'parcels'. As part of the fun, they were duly weighed, and had luggage labels tied round their necks before travelling in an old coach at the rear of the train. They retained memories of the cold, and 'terrifying' speed of the train rattling down the home run from Summit. However, they managed to make rail connections to get back to college in time to avoid trouble.

A 1953 traveller was not as lucky as someone on BR did not know that the passenger service had been withdrawn 23 years earlier. John Mallon recalled the incident, which happened when he was collecting tickets at Alnwick station from the Alnmouth train. 'A passenger approached and asked the time of the next train to Wooler. His ticket had been issued in the London area, and was made out to Wooler. He was amazed when I told him how many years it was since the service had been withdrawn. He then had to run for his bus.'

## ENDNOTES

1.    Traffic Committee, 8 September 1887.
2.    *NER Magazine*, 1911 pp. 221-4.
3.    Ibid. 1911 p. 276 also 1914 p. 253.
4.    *Alnwick Gazette*, 2 August 1919. Much later, excursion trains were run on some lines for the sole purpose of viewing the station gardens.
5.    PRO RAIL 527/1913
6.    Way and Works Committee (WW) 5 October 1885. Wooler station was not connected to the town water supply until 18 February 1930, after the stationmaster had been ill for several weeks due to poor water.
7.    WW 14 April 1895 & 2 May 1895. Charles Augustus Harrison was the nephew of T. E. Harrison.
8.    *Alnwick Gazette*, 2 January 1892.
9.    Interview with his son.
10.   R. Logan, *People and Places of Northumberland* (1945).

**CHAPTER NINE: FREIGHT SERVICES AND CLOSURE**

With very little industry on the Alnwick & Cornhill, the majority of the goods traffic was to serve the agricultural community. There was a brick and tile works at Whittingham, gravel extraction near Hedgeley and some quarry traffic at Wooler and at Summit, but none made a significant contribution to the branch's fortunes. Slaters brickworks' siding at Whittingham was removed as early as July 1915, suggesting that it made little use of the railway. Timber provided small tonnages at irregular intervals to some of the stations, and was extracted on a much larger scale during both World Wars. A special timber siding was put in near Edlingham for the use of the contractor, Robert Frazer & Sons of Hebburn, from September 1916, and another for the Timber Committee, 200 yds south of Whittingham, in 1917.[1]

During the railway's life the pattern of farming was changing with a larger acreage devoted to arable land in its early years than at its end. In Glendale over 60% of the land had been arable, but this had reduced to less than half with a corresponding increase in the less labour intensive pasture farming.[2]

The goods traffic tended to be seasonal. The peak months for the livestock traffic were during the spring and around the autumn sales in September and October. Grain, usually barley (around 3,000 tons in 1913), and root crops were exported in the autumn, and lime for the fields was imported at the same time. A full set of returns has survived for Akeld from 1887 to 1943, but the figures for the other stations, particularly after 1914, are not comprehensive.

| STATION | PASSENGER RECEIPTS £ PER ANNUM | GOODS £ PER ANNUM | TOTAL £ PER ANNUM | % OF BRANCH TOTAL |
|---|---|---|---|---|
| Wooler | 2,200 | 1,500 | 3,700 | 28.5 |
| Whittingham | 1,115 | 895 | 2,010 | 16 |
| Ilderton | 610 | 710 | 1,320 | 10.5 |
| Akeld | 480 | 770 | 1,250 | 10 |
| Hedgeley | 620 | 470 | 1,090 | 8.5 |
| Mindrum | 510 | 570 | 1,080 | 8.5 |
| Glanton | 690 | 240 | 930 | 7.5 |
| Wooperton | 420 | 355 | 775 | 6 |
| Kirknewton | 230 | 130 | 360 | 3 |
| Edlingham | 145 | 40 | 185 | 1.5 |
| TOTAL | 7,020 | 5,680 | 12,700 | 100 |

**Table 1: average station receipts from 1897 to 1914 showing the better revenue from passenger traffic. Neither the total revenue nor the figures for goods traffic are available pre-1897. Source N.R.M. Library.**

Table 1 indicates that the total receipts per mile per week, prior to 1914, came to under £7. Using T. E. Harrison's yardstick (Chapter 1) for the line to repay 5% on its investment and cover the wages' bill and the maintenance costs of the locomotives, rolling stock, signalling and permanent way, the figure should have been around £20 giving an annual total of £37,000. If we accept that the NER must have been prepared to write off the interest, the branch was still a long way short of covering its running costs. After 1914 rising wages and declining traffic made things even worse. The revenue from the passenger traffic exceeding that from the goods traffic on the branch was most unusual as, over the whole system, freight made twice as much as passengers in that period. It was not until the early 1970s, following BR's inept policies on freight rationalisation, that passenger revenue exceeded freight revenue on British Railways.

| GOODS: IN | 13,200 tons |
|---|---|
| GOODS: OUT | 10,770 tons |
| COAL, COKE, LIME | 15,780 tons |
| LIVESTOCK: IN AND OUT | 58,700 heads |

**Table 2: the average *annual* figures for goods handled, under the main headings, between 1887 and 1914. Approximately four times the number livestock was forwarded as was received. When the 'Beeching Plan' was published in 1963 the lowest category of branch line goods traffic considered was 5,000 tons per *week*.**

| STATION | LIVESTOCK HEADS IN AND OUT | COAL, COKE LIME TONS | GOODS TONS IN | GOODS TONS OUT | STATION COSTS 1900 £ |
|---|---|---|---|---|---|
| Wooler | 28,700 | 3,780 | 3,500 | 4,230 | 498 |
| Whittingham | 11,000 | 2,050 | 1,880 | 770 | 246 |
| Ilderton | 2,350 | 2,170 | 1,310 | 910 | 161 |
| Akeld | 3,430 | 1,110 | 1,250 | 1,370 | 161 |
| Hedgeley | 3,160 | 1,240 | 1,240 | 550 | 161 |
| Mindrum | 4,160 | 2,660 | 1,530 | 1,310 | 178 |
| Glanton | 630 | 1,010 | 1,060 | 290 | 167 |
| Wooperton | 2,050 | 1,200 | 860 | 630 | 172 |
| Kirknewton | 2,300 | 510 | 350 | 280 | 125 |
| Edlingham | 920 | 50 | 220 | 430 | 120 |

**Table 3: the annual average goods traffic handled by each station under the main headings from 1887 to 1914. The station costs given for 1900 include the wages of the stationmasters, signalmen, porter/signalmen and porters as appropriate. Source N.R.M. Library.**

The movement of livestock had never been a great revenue earner, but as 'Common Carriers' the railways were forced to accept any traffic, whether profitable or not, and had invested in a large fleet of wagons, manpower and facilities to handle this traffic. After the First World War, with lorries being introduced to collect animals directly from the farms, much of this traffic was soon lost from the railways. In the early 1920s sheep were already being carried on journeys over 200 miles by road. During the LNER's first decade the heads of livestock it carried in a year reduced from over 28 million, in 1923, to just 5 million. By 1928 only 2% of the total revenue for British railways was from livestock, but, now with hundreds of surplus wagons, whether this 2% included any profit is open to question. The decline continued:-

> 'Rail receipts from livestock decreased by nearly 50% between 1929 and 1939 owing to the competition of road hauliers, who carried most of the short distance traffic and a good number of sheep for distances up to 300 miles. The main requirements are a fast door to door service at low cost, and in many cases the railways cannot compete without serious dislocation of services generally.' [3]

The A&C was not hit as badly in the 1920s, serving as it did a totally agricultural area where sheep farming was on the increase. Wooler rated in the top 15 stations out of the 450 handling livestock in the North East. The branch figures for 1924 actually show a slight increase over the ones for 1913, whereas there had been a 20% decline in the whole of the North Eastern Area over the same period. However, the trend was for Wooler's share of the traffic to increase whilst the other stations on the branch handled a lot less. By the late 1930s, with the exception of the Wooler mart traffic, livestock had almost disappeared, with the total being just 15% of the 1913 figure. Appendix 2 gives the equivalent sizes for livestock.

**Plate 9.1: a general view of Wooler goods yard on 24 June 1958. A glimpse the station buildings can be seen behind the wagons on the left. The 4-ton capacity hand crane was provided some time after the line opened. The water tank is just visible to the left of the warehouse. J. F. Mallon.**

**Plate 9.2: Wooler goods warehouse and yard looking deserted in this 1958 view. The loading gauge is on the right of the picture. J. F. Mallon.**

Taking Akeld as an example of the smaller stations; in 1913 it forwarded 309 cattle, 3,025 sheep and 15 pigs, and received 400 cattle, 88 calves and 880 sheep. These required 140 wagons to be forwarded and 71 received for which £123 (8%) was included in the station's total annual receipts of £1,561. Only 61 wagons were forwarded in 1924. In 1938 it handled 853 animals in 28 wagons with receipts of £55, whereas 50 tons of game forwarded brought in £197; the total annual receipts were then down to £474. In 1947 it received 27 wagons of livestock but did not forward any at all. [4] The figures quoted become even worse if one remembers that inflation had caused wages and prices to more than quadruple by the 1930s.

People who knew the line just before its closure recalled the heavy cattle trains (around 30 wagons) that still ran for the autumn sales at Wooler. But, if we consider the true economics, less than a dozen decent train loads per year did not even justify maintaining the wagons, let alone keeping the branch open. The idea that many railwaymen had that 'any traffic was good traffic' was to be seriously revised in the 'Beeching era' after 1963.

The coming of the railway allowing the delivery of coal direct from the colliery to the local station, instead of by cart from a distant railhead, must have been a great bonus to the district. The NER, of course, cashed in on this advantage and, following its normal practice, made the stationmasters agents for the coal sales in their locality. The provision of coal cells and weighing machines in the station yard made the handling and costing of the coal and lime traffic a lot easier. The stationmasters were allowed to retain the profits from the coal sales thus making a useful addition to their basic salary. At some stations on the NER the profit from the sales even exceeded the salary! Prior to 1914 the Akeld stationmaster sold between 450 and 1,200 tons of coal per annum. His five year average for profit was £37 in 1911 and £75 by 1920. Akeld's annual report for 1930 recorded the inevitable: 'Coal being delivered into the district by motor transport.' [4] Edlingham had a small colliery nearby, at Lemmington, and this accounts for its very low figures. The import of lime for use on the fields was always seen as an important factor by people wanting a railway, but the branch had, at best, only carried a fairly insignificant tonnage and this had almost disappeared by 1910.

**Plate 9.3: the coal depot at Akeld, which allowed the rapid discharge of wagons up to a gross weight of 28½ tons provided that they were fitted with bottom doors. The station cottages and weigh office can also be seen. J. F. Mallon.**

Goods traffic forwarded included oats, barley, root crops and hay and straw, with Akeld supplying over a quarter of the branch total for these commodities. Timber was sent out at irregular intervals, both sawn and in the round, from most of the stations. Excluding the war years, the highest annual tonnage seems to have been around 2,000. In September 1917 it was reported that Canadians working a saw mill near Whittingham had 'broken all records by cutting 55,400 cubic feet of timber in a 10 hour shift. The capacity that this mill is supposed to cut is 35,000. The Canadians at Whittingham have the honour of holding the record of all such mills at work in England and Scotland.'[5]

**Plate 9.4: the interior of the goods warehouse at Wooler showing, in the right foreground, the recess in the platform to facilitate the loading and unloading of carts under cover. The office and typical farm produce and feeds are evident. There were two hand cranes in the warehouse and one in the goods yard. J. F. Mallon.**

No headings are given for the goods received at the branch stations but they must have included fertilizers, animal feeds, disinfectants and implements for the farmers as well as groceries and manufactured goods for the people of the area. Sometimes the annual returns denote a new development. The arrival of large numbers of telegraph poles at a station heralds the introduction of telephones into its area. Wagons of slag, tar or tarmac indicate that the roads are to receive a permanent surface for the first time.

As with the livestock, much of the goods traffic soon was lost to the road haulage companies. Unfortunately, no figures have come to light to show how bad things became in general, but if Akeld is considered as typical its receipts for 1938 were just £176. Allowing for inflation, this was just 3% of its average for the pre-1914 years. If the war had not come in 1939, the LNER must, surely, have seriously considered closing the branch. The staff had already been reduced to a minimum, with a stationmaster being responsible for two or three stations.

Customers sending their goods by train had the option of paying extra to have them collected from or delivered to the station by the railway company. Immediately after the passenger service was withdrawn, a lorry was garaged at Alnwick to carry the mail to Wooler and make other collections and deliveries. Soon the LNER embarked on its 'ROAD-cum-RAIL' distribution service. By the mid-1930s all the stations on the line were equipped with GPO telephones, and a list of all the villages and hamlets that could be served by each station was given in the LNER's 'Country Collection and Delivery Services' booklet. Typical *additional* rates gave one shilling for a parcel under 28 lbs and 11s-6d for a ton of goods, both carried 10 miles.[6] When the south end of the line closed in 1953 there were six railway lorries based at Alnwick.

N.S.—6/8268. 3,000. 2/12/30.

# LONDON & NORTH EASTERN RAILWAY.
## (NORTH EASTERN AREA).

.................... AKELD ....................STATION.

## TRAFFIC, Etc., for TWELVE MONTHS ended 31st DECEMBER, 1930.

| PASSENGER TRAFFIC— | LOCAL, i.e., Local to Area plus Local to Group. | Foreign. | TOTAL. | | Receipts. |
|---|---|---|---|---|---|
| Passengers Booked—......No. | 689 | .......... | 689 | £ | 36 : 10 : 2 |

| No. of 1,000 Mile Coupons exchanged for tickets issued .... | 63 |
|---|---|

| Tickets Collected ........... | To Station. 818 | To Stations Beyond. ...... | TOTAL. 818 | | |
|---|---|---|---|---|---|
| Season Tickets (Station Stock).............................. | | | | £ | : : |

**Miscellaneous Coaching Receipts :—**
(Selected Items only).

| | No. | £ | s. | d. |
|---|---|---|---|---|
| W.C.'s and Lavatories .......................... | 3 | | | |
| Platform Tickets ................................ | | | | |

| | Total Miscellaneous Receipts Net Debit | £ | : 2 : 8 |
|---|---|---|---|

| | Forwarded. | Received. |
|---|---|---|
| Parcels (under 2 cwts.) No. .................... | 506 | 598 |
| P.L.A., C.L., & D.L. No. ............. | 4 | 6 |

**Other Merchandise (2 cwts. and over) :—**
(Selected Items only).

| | Forwarded. | Received. |
|---|---|---|
| Horses (Number of Animals) .................. | 5 | 5 |
| Carriage Trucks and S.C.V.'s. (No. of Vehicles) ... | | |
| Dogs, unaccompanied ......................... | 2 | |
| Milk Cans (Full) ......................... | | |
| Fish, Fruit, etc., Tons ........................ | 16 | |
| ............................ | | |

| Parcels, Other Merchandise & Cartage Net Debit | .................... | £ 186 : 12 : 10 |
|---|---|---|

| TOTAL Debit Coaching Traffic ...................................... | £ 223 : 5 : 8 |
|---|---|

| MERCHANDISE TRAFFIC— | Forwarded. Tons. | Received. Tons. | Forwarded. Tons. | Received. Tons. |
|---|---|---|---|---|
| Collected ........... | ...... | 20 | | |
| Delivered ........... | 12 | ...... | 12 | 20 |
| Collected and Delivered | ...... | ...... | | |
| Not Carted .......... — | ...... — | ...... | 916 | 191 |
| Coal, Coke, etc....... — | ...... — | ...... | | |
| Minerals, etc. (Classes 1–6) — | ...... — | ...... | 12 | 161 |
| TOTAL .................. | | | 941 | 372 |

| Merchandise (including Coal, Mineral, and Cartage) Net Debit ............ | £ 274 : 15 : 4 |
|---|---|

| | Forwarded. | Received. | |
|---|---|---|---|
| Live Stock     Wagons.............. | 44 | 37 | £ 99 : 13 : 7 |
| Miscellaneous Receipts ...................................... | | | £ 26 : 15 : 6 |

| TOTAL Debit Merchandise, Coal, Minerals, Cartage and Live Stock Traffic and Miscellaneous Receipts ...................................... | £ 401 : 4 : 5 |
|---|---|

| TOTAL DEBIT AT STATION ...................................... | £ 624 : 10 : 1 |
|---|---|

## COAL AND COKE TRAFFIC.

|  | Tons. |
|---|---|
| Received for Retail Sale by Station Agent ............................................ | *26 ½* |
| Received consigned to Private Parties ............................................ | *72* |

## SEASON TICKET HOLDERS, 1930.

The number of Season Tickets issued by the Passenger Manager or District Passenger Manager during 1930, and accounted for through the Station Season Ticket Record Book, **together with Season Tickets issued from Station Stock if dealt with at the Station.**

| | PERIOD AVAILABLE. | | | | | | | | | | | | | | |
|---|---|---|---|---|---|---|---|---|---|---|---|---|---|---|---|
| | 1 Year | 11 mths. | 10 mths | 9 mths. | 8 mths. | 7 mths. | 6 mths. | 5 mths. | 4 mths. | 3 mths. | 2 mths. | 1 mth. | 21 days. | 14 days. | 7 days. |
| **No. of Tickets at each Period.** | | | | | FIRST CLASS. | | | | | | | | | | |
| | | | | | THIRD CLASS. | | | | | | | | | | |

| | |
|---|---|
| Station Master's Salary per annum ...... | £ *230 : 0 : 0* |
| House Rent per annum ............... | £ *19 : 10 : 0* |
| Sunday Pay per annum ............... | £     :    : |

**General Remarks by Station Agent :—**

*Passr Train Service withdrawn Sep 27ᵗᵒ*

Signature.......... *A Roberts* ..........

Date.......... *Jan 8ᵗʰ* 1931.

Summary of the traffic handled by Akeld in 1930. A. Roberts was the last stationmaster and his duties then required him to spend 2 hours each day supervising Kirknewton with the help of one of his porter/signalmen. His salary of £230 was over four times that of the first stationmaster in 1887. Earlier returns gave the total wages bill for each station, but with annual receipts of only £624 comparisons would have been somewhat disheartening at this stage.

The war provided a significant upsurge in the traffic carried. Many of the large houses and estates were adopted for military purposes. Their uses included headquarters, hospitals, schools for evacuated children, training areas together with munitions, fuel and food stores. A fighter airfield built at Milfield gave Akeld a new lease of life. Timber and sand and gravel were needed in vast quantities for war defences, and heavy trains carrying both were frequently dispatched from the line. Mary Brown, of Whittingham, recalled: 'At some of the small stations, one could see tanks, trees, cattle, flour, slag, lime and grain being put on rail or off-loaded – civilians and military milling around – truly an amazing scene when one considers the facilities and staff available.' [7]

**Plate 9.5: the collapse of the bridge No. 42 north of Ilderton in October 1949 resulted in the branch being worked as two sections: Alnwick - Ilderton and Coldstream - Wooler. J. F. Mallon.**

Within months of the war ending the goods handled reverted to a few livestock, some small tonnages of coal and little else. The Labour government was elected in 1945, and with its immediate plans to nationalize most industries, the railway companies were not going to make any decisions on closing branches. The unwieldy British Transport Commission came into being on 1 January 1948, with the Railway Executive controlling the railways.

On 12 August 1948, less than eight months into the new regime's tenure, extreme flooding caused damage to the railways around the eastern Scottish border (see Chapter 11). The Alnwick & Cornhill lost two bridges between Mindrum and Kirknewton, and other parts of the trackbed were damaged or buried under debris. If anything should have sounded the death knell of the branch, this should. However, the only immediate economy was to close Edlingham from autumn 1948.[8]

With the line severed, Mindrum was served from Coldstream, and trains ran from Alnwick to Kirknewton. It was on one of the latter that John Mallon made his first footplate trip over the line in September 1949, soon after he started work as a clerk at Alnwick station. He recalled that a red flag was placed between the rails, just an engine length beyond the points at Kirknewton station, so that the class J39 could run round its train. A little over a month later this trip was to become impossible. On the night of 25/26 October 1949, the bridge over the Lilburn Burn, just north of Ilderton, was washed out (see Chapter 11). With Alnwick trains unable to get any further than Ilderton, and Wooler, Akeld and Kirknewton now without trains could the branch remain open? Amazingly, a decision was made to repair the track and bridges at the north end of the line. The service from Coldstream to Wooler re-commenced on 5 December 1949 subject to a 10mph speed limit. In the meantime lorries had handled the remaining traffic from nearby railheads.

Plate 9.6: class D20 4-4-0 No. 62371 waiting for the penultimate Alnwick–Ilderton parcels train to be loaded or unloaded at Ilderton on 27 February 1953. J. W. Armstrong.

Plate 9.7: the last parcels train from Alnwick to Ilderton at Hedgeley on 28 February 1953 hauled by a class J39 locomotive. The empty goods wagons will be left for loading recovered track and other equipment during the following week from the north end of this section. The group next to the locomotive are L to R; fireman R. Blacklock, guard Dixon, J. F. Mallon and driver R. Carson. J. M. Fleming.

**Plate 9.8: the return trip of the same train attracted some attention at Wooperton. A small flag is carried on the top lamp iron. J. M. Fleming.**

The parcels and goods trains between Alnwick and Ilderton were soon combined, but the traffic was negligible. The Transport Users' Consultative Committee approved the closure of that half of the line at a special meeting in January 1953. The three rural councils of Alnwick, Glendale and Rothbury naturally raised objections. One councillor justified keeping the line open because 'a few years ago [1947], during severe storms, the railway was the only means of supplying bread to the Ilderton area'! British Railways said that the cost of restoring the bridge at Ilderton would be prohibitive in relation to the traffic receipts, and that the credit from removing the track and other assets would be £50,000. The Railway's lorries based at Alnwick would handle what remained of the parcels and freight traffic.[9] The service was withdrawn from 2 March 1953. The last goods train ran on Saturday 28 February from Ilderton to Alnwick with John Mallon on the footplate. He wrote; -

> 'There were people at all the stations to see it pass. Small flags were flown on the train, and detonators were exploded as it pulled out of each station for the last time. Demolition started at Ilderton on the following Monday, the material being taken away by rail. The work was completed in February 1954, with a short length of track being left at Alnwick for siding accommodation.'

One valuable asset was bridge No. 59 over the River Breamish, at 22m-4chs just north of Hedgeley station; it was of wrought-iron lattice construction, and in very good condition (plate 3.4). The twin hog-backed main girders were 104ft-8in long, 10ft-2in high at mid-span and 2ft-3in wide. They were considered worth removing intact by rail for re-use near Wakefield. The cross-girders and decking were removed and the main girders were moved together and tied to retain lateral stability. A trestle was erected in the centre of the river, and with the aid of 3in diameter steel balls on it and the south abutment the girders were rolled until in a position to be lifted on to wagons by steam cranes (plate 9.10).[10]

Kirknewton station closed a month after the southern section, on 30 March 1953. Wooler, Akeld and Mindrum lingered a further 12 years until 29 March 1965, when the Beeching axe finally fell on the line. The Tweedmouth–Coldstream–St. Boswells freight service ceased on the same day. The last train ran from Wooler to Coldstream on 25 March hauled by B. R. standard class 3 mogul No. 77002. Within a year the entire track had been removed by BR contractors, giving a net profit on the scrap recovered of about £2,000 per mile.

**Plate 9.9: J25 0-6-0 No. 65727 at Wooler with a freight from Coldstream on 17 August 1953. Driver T. Pacey, fireman D. Thompson (on tender), guard C. Walker and a little girl on the footplate. J. F. Mallon.**

**Plate 9.10: the bridge over the River Breamish being rolled southwards prior to its removal as an out-of-gauge load to its new home in the West Riding.**

## ENDNOTES

1. NER Siding Agreements. Frazer's siding was terminated in July 1919.
2. AE Smailes, *North England* (1960) pp. 262-3.
3. H F Sanderson, *Rly Commercial Practice Vol. 2* (1952) p.104.
4. Annual returns for Akeld station. Private collection.
5. Local newspapers.
6. LNER, *Country Collection and Delivery Services by Motor* (1937) pp. 50-2.
7. Aln and Breamish Local History Society Vol. 1 No. 6 (1973) p.17.
8. Goods Manager's circular 22/1948 stated: 'The lines and connections at Edlingham have been removed and all truck loads of traffic previously dealt with at the Siding should in future be labelled and invoiced to Whittingham. "Smalls" traffic should be sent to Alnwick and invoiced to Whittingham. Whittingham rates should be charged in all cases.'
9. *Alnwick Gazette*, 23 and 30 January 1953.
10. *Modern Transport,* 18 September 1954 p.13.

# CHAPTER TEN: SIGNALLING
## By John Mallon and Chris Woolstenholmes.

At the time of its construction, the A&C was a rare example, in the North East at least, of a line subject to the requirements of no less than 10 pieces of legislation affecting the working of railways and the provision of safety appliances. Principal among these, as far as signalling was concerned, was the Railway Regulation Act (Returns of Signal Arrangements, Working, etc.), 1873,which by Section 4, required railway companies to make annual returns to the Board of Trade showing progress made in respect of block telegraph and single line working. In effect, therefore, this Act, and its predecessor, the Railway Regulation Act, 1871, ensured that the A&C would not be permitted to open for passenger trains to run until all the requirements regarding signalling had been complied with, and formally inspected and approved by an officer from the Railway Department of the B.O.T.

| SIGNAL CABIN | No. of working levers | No. of spare |
|---|---|---|
| Alnwick North | 9 | 3 |
| Summit | 14 | 4 |
| Edlingham | 20 | 5 |
| Whittingham | 19 | 3 |
| Glanton | 22 | 4 |
| Hedgeley | 26 | 2 |
| Wooperton | 21 | 1 |
| Ilderton | 22 | 4 |
| Wooler South | 15 | 3 |
| Wooler North | 11 | 3 |
| Akeld | 20 | 2 |
| Kirknewton | 20 | 4 |
| Mindrum | 22 | 4 |
| Coldstream South | 6 | 4 |

**Signalling details from Major-General Hutchinson's report for the Board of Trade prior to the opening of the line, dated 30 August 1887. He stated: 'In addition to the above there are, as a rule in each level crossing cabin, which is not a station, 6 working levers and 2 spare ones.'**

Details of the signalling contractors and costs have already been discussed on page 48. When the line opened, it was divided into eleven single-line sections of varying lengths, but typically averaging 3 miles. Each was controlled by the Train Staff & Ticket system coupled with the telegraph. 'One passenger train and one goods or two goods' were permitted to pass each other at Summit, Edlingham, Hedgeley, Ilderton, Akeld and Mindrum. At Whittingham, Wooler and Kirknewton passenger or goods could pass.[1] Wooperton and Glanton were what the NER termed 'preceding places', where a train might be signalled into the loop line for a following train overtake and precede it to the next station.

Three years after the passing of the Light Railways Act, 1896, and less than twelve years after the line opened, authority was given, in August 1899, to simplify the signalling.[2] This was completed by 1901 when the cabins at Edlingham, Glanton, Wooperton, Akeld, and Mindrum were closed and replaced by dwarf frames at a cost of £806. The new Stevens & Sons dwarf frames were placed in extensions to the stations' verandahs; the telegraph instruments were transferred to the booking offices (plates 10.1, 10.3). The signalmen were reduced in grade to porter/signalmen. The next step was the closure of Coldstream South cabin on 5 March 1904, when the Staff Section was extended to Coldstream cabin, which then controlled the junction with the A&C.

On 27 July 1908, the four signal boxes south of and including Whittingham were equipped with Electric Train Staff machines, and in 1912 the Whittingham to Hedgeley was similarly equipped. The latter possibly used the machines which became available when Summit cabin closed in late 1911. Summit had controlled a short passing loop, holding an engine, a van and 9 wagons, and the building was then used as a platelayers' accommodation until demolished in the late 1930s (plate 10.2).

**Plate 10.1: the Stevens & Sons dwarf frame at Akeld seen from inside the verandah on 25 June 1958. J. F. Mallon.**

**Plate 10.2: Signalman Peter Salmon at Summit cabin. This view, looking towards Edlingham, was taken just before its closure in 1911. The box superstructure was similar to the type used for bridge cabins (examples survive at Wylam and Hexham). J. F. Mallon collection.**

Following current practice when the line was opened, the lamps and spectacles were placed on the signal posts a short distance below the arms. After Grouping, it was decided to implement a programme of fixing Distant signals at Caution on lightly-used lines in order to reduce maintenance costs. For example, Akeld was simplified in 1926, and the Distant signal conversion programme had been completed by 1930.[3] Prior to 1924 the signals controlling the goods yard at Kirknewton were dispensed with and movements in and out of the sidings were hand-signalled. In 1924 Kirknewton ceased to be a block post and all the signals were removed; seven levers of the original 24 were retained to work the points, facing point locks and a clearance bar. In 1926, an eight-lever frame, unlocked by a key attached to the Staff, was provided to work the layout. When Edlingham ceased to be a block post and became an unstaffed halt on 14 December 1925, its signals were taken down and the dwarf frame controlled the only remaining turnouts. When Alnwick North closed on 27 May 1930, the ETS instruments were replaced by Electric Key Token machines, which themselves succumbed to Tyer's No. 6 Tablet machines on 27 February 1936. Earlier, on 15 February 1932, Mindrum and Ilderton ceased to be block posts and Electric Staff Sections were introduced from Hedgeley to Wooler, Wooler to Akeld and Akeld to Coldstream.[4]

| STAFF OR TABLET STATIONS AND SECTIONS. | REMARKS. (Also see paras. 1, 2 and 3, above). | Persons authorised to receive a tablet staff or ticket from or deliver it to the driver. | For Regulations, see pages |
|---|---|---|---|
| **Alnwick and Coldstream.** | | | |
| ALNWICK AND *WHITTINGHAM. (Electric Key token). | **Whittingham.**—Trains may pass each other at Whittingham. | Signalman at Alnwick. | Electric Tablet Regulations. |
| *WHITTINGHAM AND *HEDGELEY. (Electric staff with Blue handle). | **Hedgeley.**—Trains may pass each other at Hedgeley. | Station Master or Porter Signalman at Whittingham. | |
| *HEDGELEY AND *ILDERTON. (Staff with square handle and tickets). | **Ilderton.**—Trains may pass each other at Ilderton. | Station Master or Porter Signalman at Hedgeley. | |
| *ILDERTON AND WOOLER. (Staff with round handle and tickets). | **Wooler.**—Trains may pass each other at Wooler. | Station Master or Porter Signalman at Ilderton. | |
| WOOLER AND *AKELD. (Staff with crosshead handle and tickets) | **Akeld.**—Trains may pass each other at Akeld. | Signalman or Porter Signalman at Wooler. | 3–9 |
| *AKELD AND *MINDRUM. (Staff with square handle and tickets). | **Mindrum.**—Trains may pass each other at Mindrum. | Station Master or Porter Signalman at Akeld. | |
| | | Station Master or Porter Signalman at Mindrum. | |
| *MINDRUM AND COLDSTREAM. (Staff with round handle and tickets). | .   .   .   .   . | Signalman at Coldstream. | |

**Details of the single line sections from the LNER (North Eastern Area) Appendix to the Working Time Table dated 1 June 1931. Passing places are denoted by an asterisk. The different colour and shape of the Staff was a Board of Trade requirement to seek to prevent the use of the wrong staff on an adjoining section.**

On 11 July 1923, the cabin Brewery Road crossing, just south of Wooler station, was replaced by a five-lever Stevens ground frame on the north side of the crossing. The gates were worked sympathetically by hand (instead of by a gate wheel), and the gatekeeper was replaced by a platelayer's wife who lived in an adjacent railway house. Her attention was drawn to the approach of a train by the ringing of a bell placed on the house wall.

Early in 1926, with the serious decline in traffic, the LNER Area Board reviewed the working of the branch and sought further economies in the control of level crossings. The success at Brewery Road prompted them to propose to replace gatemen by lower-paid gate women (usually platelayers' wives) at eight crossings. At two locations, it was decided to abolish the crossing cabins, and at Learchild, where it was thought there was no obligation to work the gates, hand-worked field gates, protected by signals worked by a two-lever ground frame, were substituted. These measures, which were estimated to give annual savings of £288 in maintenance and £979 in wages, were approved on 22 April 1926.[5]

On 15 February 1932 further alterations were made to the level crossings at Roseden, Wooler Haugh, Brewery Road, Wooler South, Bendor, Yeavering, Kirknewton, Kilham Siding, Langham Bridge and Hagg. The existing signalling was dispensed with and Caution Boards, fitted with two yellow lights, and fixed 600 yards on either side of the crossings, were brought into use. The boards were lettered 'Level Crossing, Whistle, 10 mph' (plate 10.9). Drivers of all trains on approaching them had to reduce their speed from the line limit of 25 mph to 10 mph, and be prepared to find the level crossing gates across the railway.[6] The cost of the boards was £346 but the savings claimed were only £24 per annum. [5]

By August 1955, the gatekeepers had been withdrawn north of Wooler and the gates were worked by the train crews (plate 10.7). Some time between 1957 and 1960, the Coldstream-Akeld ETS system was superseded by Tyer's No. 6 Tablet machines with C (triangular) configuration. Akeld-Wooler became a 'One Engine in Steam' section. These arrangements lasted until the line's closure in 1965.

### ENDNOTES

1. Appendix to the Working Timetable in force from 1 January 1908.
2. Traffic Committee Minute 31 August 1899. The Light Railway Act with its lower standards for lightly used lines may have acted as a prompt for the NER to reduce its standards on similar branches.
3. PRO RAIL 398/286.
4. LNER (North Eastern Area) Permanent Way Programme No. 4, 1932.
5. PRO RAIL 390/169.
6. LNER (NE Area) Permanent Way Programme No. 4 1932 page 81.
7. PRO RAIL 390/61.

**Plate 10.3: Glanton station, looking towards Wooler, c. 1905, showing the 1887 cabin boarded up, and its 1901 successor situated in the extension to the verandah to the right of the lady on the platform. The signal lamps are now positioned level with the arms. The two arms of signal 3 on the left read from the platform line to the goods yard or up starting. The top arms, co-acting main up home signals to loop line or platform line, are just discernable against the sky background. C. J. Woolstenholmes collection.**

**Plate 10.4: D20 No. 62371, on the penultimate parcels train on the southern end, running round its train at Hedgeley on 27 February 1953. The driver is about to receive the Train Staff from the signalman. Note this cabin, which controlled a level crossing, is narrower and longer than others on the line. J. W. Armstrong.**

## SIGNALLING DIAGRAMS

### SUMMIT SIDING 1887

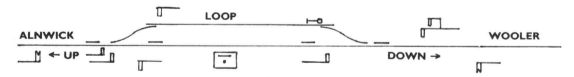

### EDLINGHAM STATION 1901

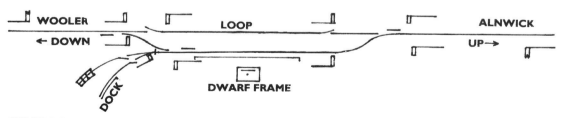

### TYPICAL LEVEL CROSSING

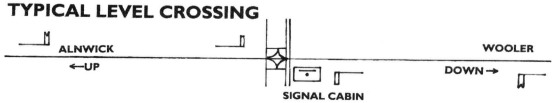

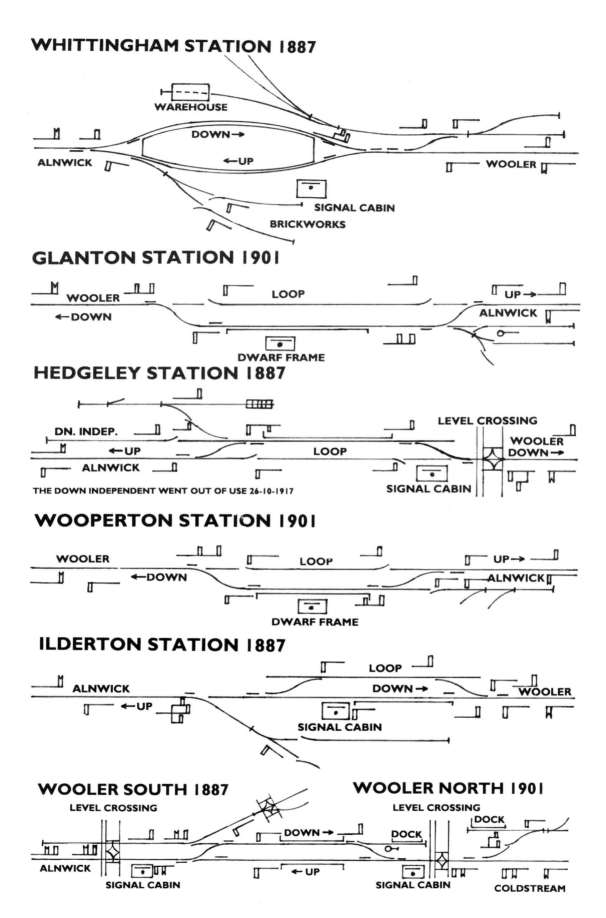

# WHITTINGHAM STATION 1887

WAREHOUSE
DOWN →
← UP
ALNWICK
WOOLER
SIGNAL CABIN
BRICKWORKS

# GLANTON STATION 1901

WOOLER
← DOWN
LOOP
UP →
ALNWICK
DWARF FRAME

# HEDGELEY STATION 1887

DN. INDEP.
← UP
ALNWICK
LOOP
LEVEL CROSSING
WOOLER
DOWN →
SIGNAL CABIN

THE DOWN INDEPENDENT WENT OUT OF USE 26-10-1917

# WOOPERTON STATION 1901

WOOLER
← DOWN
LOOP
UP →
ALNWICK
DWARF FRAME

# ILDERTON STATION 1887

ALNWICK
← UP
LOOP
DOWN →
WOOLER
SIGNAL CABIN

# WOOLER SOUTH 1887

LEVEL CROSSING
DOWN →
ALNWICK
SIGNAL CABIN
← UP

# WOOLER NORTH 1901

LEVEL CROSSING
DOCK
DOCK
SIGNAL CABIN
COLDSTREAM

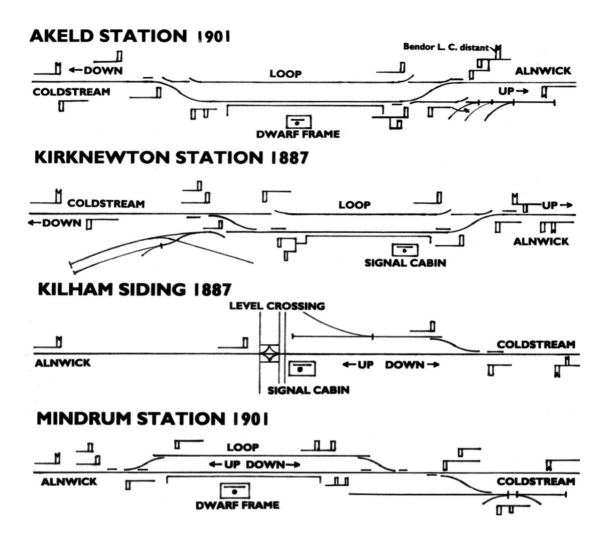

## AKELD STATION 1901

←DOWN
COLDSTREAM
LOOP
Bendor L. C. distant
ALNWICK
UP→
DWARF FRAME

## KIRKNEWTON STATION 1887

COLDSTREAM
←DOWN
LOOP
UP→
ALNWICK
SIGNAL CABIN

## KILHAM SIDING 1887

LEVEL CROSSING
ALNWICK
COLDSTREAM
←UP   DOWN→
SIGNAL CABIN

## MINDRUM STATION 1901

LOOP
←UP  DOWN→
ALNWICK
COLDSTREAM
DWARF FRAME

**Plate 10.5: this enamel signal cabin nameplate survived at least until August 1953, when it was photographed attached to one of the cottages at Summit. J. F. Mallon.**

Plate 10.6: an early picture, looking north-east of Kilham Siding cabin, with the white oval-shaped plate on its front elevation indicating that the block telegraph is in working order. Note that four gates have been provided for this single-vehicle width road. D. J. Williamson collection.

Plate 10.7: 60 years after the picture above, the gates are being opened at Kilham Sidings, seen looking north-west over the tender of J25 No. 65727. Two gates have replaced the four, and the signal cabin has been demolished, but a typical gatekeeper's cottage remains on the left.
J. F. Mallon 22 August 1953.

**Plate 10.8: the former Haugh Head cabin, south of Wooler, in use as holiday accommodation after that end of the branch had been lifted. J. M. Fleming.**

**Plate 10.9: the north-bound warning board for Langham Bridge level crossing facing the camera with the back of Kilham Siding's for the up direction seen beyond. J. F. Mallon 25 June 1958.**

**Plate10.10: Whittingham cabin in 1953 after the frame was removed, showing the access door to the locking room under the steps and no porch. J. W. Armstrong.**

**Plate 11.1: J39 No. 64868 being re-railed on 10 July 1953 after this incident at the points at the site of Alnwick North. J. F. Mallon.**

## CHAPTER ELEVEN: INCIDENTS AND EPHEMERA

During its 80 years of use the branch had a number of incidents, the major ones being caused by weather. Many of the happenings were recorded in the local newspapers, but some were gleaned by John Mallon from his conversations with old timers, over a span of 50 years. Some stories, which, at first, he did not believe, turned out to be true when checked with the Train Registers and other documents that were available before the branch was closed.

### Weather

In 1886, during the construction of the line heavy snow had delayed the work, but the first winter of the railway's operations was to show how bad it could be. The snowfalls of the second week in March 1888 were worse than any experienced for many years. On Thursday 15th the main line to Edinburgh was blocked north and south of Alnmouth, but the evening train from Coldstream got through to Alnwick. It had arrived at Summit in a very creditable hour-and-a half, but took another 45 minutes to cover the last 4 miles *down* the 1 in 50 gradient. Many of the platelayers had joined the train at the stations between Wooler and Alnwick, and their shovels were needed to clear the cuttings near Summit. The resolute engine crew, Edward Capsticks and Robert Young, reported drifts up to six feet deep with some lengthy stretches with three feet of snow. The last down train left Alnwick on Thursday evening, but a carriage and van were forced off the line by the hard packed snow at Wooperton. The locomotive had to detach these and another carriage before it could make any progress. Two engines and 40 men had to be despatched from Berwick on Friday morning to clear the line. In January 1889 the main line was blocked north of Newcastle, but there is no record of the branch being closed.

In November 1893 the worst gales for 12 years were to affect the line. The trains 'were all running very late owing to the storm retarding their progress. The driver of the mid-day train on this branch had a narrow escape through a tree having been blown over on to railway near to Percy's Cross [NU 054193] while the train was running past it.'

**Plate 11.2: clearing the debris at Akeld station left by flooding during the last week in April 1906. A similar scene occurred here in August 1948. J. Newbegin NERA.**

In the last week of April 1906 nearly five inches of rain were recorded in the area, and the inevitable flooding caused moderately severe damage to the line. A small subsidence near Summit was quickly repaired, but the worst damage was beyond Wooler where the Cheviot burns caused havoc. The Humbleton and Akeld Burns both washed away lengths of the railway embankment, and similar damage was caused at Yeavering. Akeld station office was flooded, and a considerable amount of debris was deposited on the track (plate 11.2). On Saturday 28 April Wooler to Kirknewton was impassable, but the breakdown gangs working through until Monday lunchtime allowed the 1-45pm train from Alnwick to reach Coldstream.

.Although there were many bad winters and storms, the notorious blizzards of 1947 together with the floods of the following year really made the headlines. The snowfalls of early 1947 were considered to be worse than those of 1888. From 1902 two snow ploughs had been allocated to Alnmouth. Fortunately, during the first week in February 1947, these were used several times in order to keep the line clear of drifting snow. (A jet engine, mounted on a wagon, was tried to clear the snow, but soon derailed itself opposite Alnwick sawmills.) Had the ploughs not been used, and the line abandoned to the snow, things could have become even more serious for the district as the weather got worse over the next four weeks. All road transport in Northumberland was reported to have been brought to a complete standstill, and the fickle public were again dependent on the railways for food and coal supplies. Without the railway Wooler, and many of the villages, would have been totally cut off for over 10 days.

**Plate 11.3: a snow scene at Whittingham in 1947. J. F. Mallon collection.**

The situation could not have been much worse as, after six years of war and with food and fuel rationing still in force, no one had well-stocked larders and coal cellars to carry them through a prolonged cold spell. However, humanity prevailed and, for example, Girl Guides were allowed to take coal from Hedgeley station on sledges to the homes of the elderly around Powburn. 'At Wooler station people arrived with tractors, trailers and sledges to seek coal.' The railway even helped to bring entertainment: 'Wooler cinema received its films by train, but otherwise all other social functions have been cancelled.' This spell of weather caused Glendale Council to consider petitioning B. R. to *permanently* reinstate the passenger service. How much use would it have had? One passenger train had been run at the start of the blizzards to rescue people stranded in the district.

On 12 August 1948 prolonged, torrential rain fell on the Lammermuir Hills and the area to the south of them. The scale of the downpour was such that the streams and rivers were totally inadequate to cope. They soon burst their banks, and, as the volume of water increased, damage to bridges and property ensued. The railways and roads of the eastern Borders were very badly hit. Seven bridges on the East Coast Main Line between Berwick and Dunbar were washed out. The Eyemouth and Berwickshire lines both lost bridges, and on the A&C two were damaged between Mindrum and Kirknewton. One of the bridges, No. 16 an 11 feet span wrought-iron trough girder bridge at 5m-65chs, over Kilham Burn, was destroyed and No. 23, a two span wrought-iron girder bridge over the College burn, just west of Kirknewton was severely damaged. Fortunately, the Kelso Branch only needed minor repairs as it had to be used by diverted express trains until the main-line bridges were replaced. The *Flying Scotsman*, diverted from Tweedmouth via Kelso and the Waverley line, still managed a number of non-stop runs between the capitals.

**Plate 11.4: temporary bridge No. 16 over the Kilham Burn. This replacement and that of No. 23, damaged in the 1948 floods, allowing the line to re-open between Coldstream and Wooler after the October 1949 damage to bridge No. 42 at Ilderton. J. F. Mallon.**

Instead of using the flood damage as an excuse to close the line, B. R. decided to work the Mindrum traffic from Coldstream and the remainder of the branch from Alnwick. Many accounts that have appeared about the damage to the branch confuse that caused by the floods of 1948 and 1949. On 25/26 October 1949, the Lilburn Burn, which was fed by streams rising 1,300 feet above sea level, on the east flank of the Cheviot, was swollen by heavy rainfall driven by ferocious winds. The foundations of the 30 feet span wrought-iron bridge No. 42, just north of Ilderton station, were scoured away by the flood causing an abutment to collapse. The floods of the previous year, which had destroyed the neighbouring road bridge, may have weakened the foundation, but as scour is extremely difficult to detect this would have gone unnoticed.[1] The ballast between Ilderton and Wooler 'was also considerably disturbed.'

After the 1948 damage, the permanent way inspector had been quietly tipping ballast to repair the damaged embankments and stabilise the track between Mindrum and Kilham Sidings. When someone in authority heard of this he was told to stop, but events were to prove him right. As explained in Chapter 9, the bridges and track between Mindrum and Kirknewton had to be repaired, allowing Wooler to be served from the north end. The track between the Lilburn Burn and Wooler was left in situ until the north end of the line was lifted, by which time it had become very overgrown. Wooler South's level crossing gates were permanently open to road traffic from 4 September 1950.

**Incidents**

The only known injury to a member of the public happened before the line was opened to passengers. Mrs. English, the wife of a joiner, was awarded '£125 including medical and other expenses' for injuries she received at Hedgeley station on 25 June 1887. Her husband had claimed £200 on her behalf.[2]

On 22 January 1895 the 10-30am passenger train from Coldstream had one of the springs for a leading tender wheel break, causing both wheels to leave the rails. The train was on the final down gradient beyond Summit, and as it took some distance to stop there was considerable damage to the rail chairs. The derailment was reported immediately to Summit signal cabin, and a telegraph message was sent to Alnwick. Mr. Patterson, the stationmaster there, sent a train carrying a number of workmen to the scene, and the same train carried the passengers on to Alnwick. The 1-50pm return passenger train certainly did not run, but it is not recorded how soon the line was cleared and repaired. One of the passengers delayed at Alnwick was the Earl of Ravensworth en route for his seat, Eslington Park, Whittingham.

The 1 in 50 gradients on each side of the summit on Alnwick Moor were always going to cause problems in operating the line, with 'greasy' rails and badly steaming locomotives often bringing trains to a standstill. The maximum freight train tonnages laid down for each class of locomotives on this section ranged from only 115 tons for the class O (G5) 0-4-4T to 235 tons for the large 0-8-0 classes. The class R (D20) 4-4-0s were allowed 130 tons for freight and 157 tons for passenger trains. Freight trains were allowed 20 to 30 minutes to cover the 4m-26c from Alnwick to Summit.[3] The heaviest load ever taken by a single locomotive may have been on 22 April 1943. Ex-NBR 0-6-0 class J37 No. 9123, driven by Billy Black and fired by Claude Isham, took 39 wagons from Alnwick to Whittingham. Driver Black said they had no difficulties with the load. Other footplate men recalled 20 wagons as a normal load. The classes of locomotives used on the line are given in Appendix 5.

There must have been many incidents of stalled trains needing assistance up these gradients. In March 1895 an irate passenger, whose 7-10am train from Wooler had stalled on no less than three days in the previous week approaching Summit, complained to the Newcastle newspaper. He signed himself as 'One who Always Drives to Alnwick when Possible' – no doubt only using the trains in inclement weather. He thought stalling on the bank was dangerous because 'the brakes may refuse to act.' The NER passenger trains were all now fitted with the safe and efficient Westinghouse air brakes. He was also aggrieved that the line went over Alnwick Moor instead of up the Aln Valley to Eglingham, and claimed everyone was paying an unnecessary extra two pence for the longer journey.

In a later example, a northbound troop train stalled on 31 October 1939, and required assistance from D20 No. 1078. However, the most notorious happened on 8 March 1941 when the main line was bombed near Belford. The 10-05am express from York to Edinburgh was diverted, by some genius at control, over the A&C. A3 Pacific *Bayardo* was in charge of the train, which probably had a wartime loading of around 500 tons. The engine needed to run round at Alnwick, and, because of the train's length, this took an awful lot of manoeuvring in the station yard. The train did not leave until 3-46pm, long after it should have been in Edinburgh. The 50 feet diameter turntable at the station was much too small to turn a Pacific, so the A3 left running tender first with Alnmouth driver, Bob Jamieson, at the regulator. It was assisted by D20 No. 592 driven by John Connell. According to the permitted loadings, the maximum that the two locomotives should take was under 400tons. Needless to say, they did not make it up the gradient. At 5-37pm the guard arrived back at Alnwick on foot to say that the train was well and truly stuck on the bank. Another D20 No. 2023, driven by George Barratt that was attached to the parcels train was sent to assist in the rear. The three locomotives made slow but steady progress over the summit. At Whittingham No. 2023 was uncoupled, but the driver was asked to push up the 1 in 66 gradient to Glanton, until the express pulled ahead. Whittingham was left at 6-43pm, and Hedgeley was passed at 6-55pm, and, still double-headed, the express arrived at Tweedmouth around 8-15pm. The passengers would have been lucky to have made Edinburgh much before 10-0pm. No. 2023, with its parcels vans, had to go through to Coldstream, but it made record time back to Alnwick, arriving at 10-23pm. Reputedly, it was travelling so fast that a piece of the ceiling in one of the station cottages en route was dislodged by the vibrations.[4] John Mallon found out later that it was the station master at Alnwick who got a reprimand for the delays, and not the clown in control who had sent a heavy express on to a steeply graded freight-only line, which had no facilities to deal with it.[5]

In another war-time incident, a twin-engined aircraft came down on the line 150yds south of Mossy Ford (NU 165110) on 10 May 1942. According to the Train Register, the branch was re-opened at 3-5pm the following day.

**Newspaper Quotes 1887-1919 (from the *Alnwick Gazette* unless stated otherwise) Researched by Vera Mallon.**

COACH TO BE DISCONTINUED: 17 September 1887
'The coach between Wooler and Belford [station] is about to be discontinued, after eleven years of service. Mr. Bertram, the proprietor of the coach, deserves the thanks of the community in general for the long continued service to the public during the term of years. The carrier at Berwick, who went twice a week, finished his last journey yesterday. Thus it is, both coaches and carriers' carts that must yield to the more expeditious way of transit by rail.'

'The opening of the new auction mart at Wooler was a great success last Monday. Wooler in the olden times was famous for its fairs and cattle markets. In the days of cattle markets without a railway, Wooler has been left out in the cold. Judging from the business done on Monday, and the efficient way which the new auctioneer discharged it, there seems to be a glorious future for Wooler Auction Mart.'
WOOLER NEWS: 8 October 1887
'By the opening of the new railway, our shopkeepers are getting wakened up and keeping pace with the times. Some of our shop windows are very credibly decorated, and attract the attention of the passers-by, and will bear favourable comparison with any town of the same size. Two additional refreshment rooms, to be conducted on temperance principles, have recently opened so that tourists, visitors and persons attending the Auction Marts will find an abundant supply of substantial and suitable food for them, as well as in the old established and well-known hostelries and refreshment rooms in the town.'
'ANY MORE FOR THE WEST? 10 December 1887
'This cry is certainly comparatively curious to the people of this town, and was evidently indistinguishably so to the pair of "canny" cattle farmers who arrived at the Alnwick terminus on Tuesday evening by express train, intending to journey on the new Cornhill branch. The express was late, and the Cornhill train was waiting its arrival. Out jumped the two gentlemen, spoken of, while the cry of the railway official rang out with stentorian vehemence, and reverberated through the arcaded structure – "any more for the west?"'
'The bucolic "bodies" stood the while at the barrier, talking to and gesticulating with a local butcher, paying no heed to the repeated vociferations "any more for the west?" until the train to Cornhill was observed by one of them, gliding smoothly out of the station, several minutes after time. "Is that the 'Ooler train?" he gasped to the porter, "Ay, that's hor" was the response'. They had to stay the night in Alnwick. The journalist suggested the cry 'train t'ooler!, train t'ooler!' would be better understood by the locals!
DESCRIPTION OF THE COUNTRY: *The Graphic*, 14 January 1888
Around the time that the railway was opened local newspapers gave accounts of the facts leading to the completion of the line, which have been covered in our earlier chapters. Soon the fine scenery and turbulent history of the area were to be featured in newspapers, in articles by journalists and correspondents. The following extract from *The Graphic,* even with its inaccuracies, gives the flavour of the district.
'The railway passes through a most interesting part of England, comprehending within its route, beautiful scenery in the Vales of the Aln, the Breamish and the Till, reaching right on until it joins the Tweed at Cornhill. Whittingham Vale, which opens up after passing Edlingham, the first station, six miles from Alnwick, is one of the most lovely in Northumberland, and one full of delightful attractions, and when we add the attractions of

Coquetdale and of Glendale, all within easy range, we have a stretch of country which might well be termed *una terra mareviliosa.*'

'Here are the great mountain ranges crowned by the Cheviot [2674ft], surrounded by lesser hills, all having their own special beauties, and the most extensive prospects. All along their summits, on their sides, and in the valleys also, are to be found endless traces of a populous pre-historic occupation by men whose methods of life can only be guessed at. Ancient British settlements, British towns, and burial places, localities where occur those mysterious rock-markings and incised stones, said to be symbols of a worship which once prevailed all over the world, now obsolete here, though still lingering in our far-off possessions in the East; unmistakeable evidence of Watling Street, that wonderful specimen of Roman construction, here called "the Devil's Causeway", entrenchments on the hills, and protective stations in the valleys.'

**Plate 11.5: this view of Kirknewton station looking over the River Glen to the foothills of the Cheviot gives an idea of the superb but rugged scenery. J. F. Mallon collection.**

'The Saxon left his records in the names of the villages and homesteads, and the Norman built his castles, Pele towers and Bastle houses, to protect himself from the predatory Scot. Eslington was a crenellated mansion in 1336, and Callaly was in the possession of the Claverings (who claim descent from Charlemagne) for six hundred years. Lorbottle dates back to the time of Henry II (1177). Chillingham Castle, consisting of four massive towers, built in the thirteenth century, since enlarged, has now an Elizabethan character imparted to it. Its wild cattle, said to be descendants from the ancient breed of the country which roamed along "the backbone of hills reaching from Cheviot to Hamilton" can be seen on a clear day from Ilderton Station on the line, disporting themselves on Roscastle Hill, at the foot of which the castle is built.'

'Wooler is about mid-way between Alnwick and Cornhill, and is placed in a most charming situation within easy distance of some of the most remarkable spots in the locality; spots where men made history in a way wherein rugged strength most prevailed. The field of Hedgeley Moor, where the Percy, Sir Hugh, when dying, exclaimed, "I have saved the bird in my breast!", meaning that he had kept the oath to Henry VI, is about six miles from Wooler.'

'The battle field of Flodden, in Milfield Plain, lies about eight miles to the north-west of Wooler, and about three miles from Mindrum Station; and Ford Castle is near, where King

James slept on the night before the battle, "When shiver'd was fair Scotland's spear, And broken was her shield".'

'Beginning at Alnwick, with its princely castle, "the Windsor of the North", and its many attractions, until we get to Coldstream on the other side of the Tweed, we are carried along a breadth of country which for natural beauty, grandeur of scenery, historical interest, antiquarian allurements dear to the "Oldbucks" of our generation' and fishing enticements for our Izaac Walton's, it would be difficult to find excelled elsewhere.'

The railway was not to benefit everyone as the following indicate:

GOOD FOR ALNWICK? 22 October 1887

'Has the new railway done any good for Alnwick? This is a question one hears often asked; many, with a significant shake of the head, give themselves up to very gloomy forebodings, others again are quite confident that it will eventually be a boon here. One thing is beyond doubt, we do not see the long string of country carts we used to witness at various public-house doors. They are effectually "run off". I hear great complaints about the considerable delay and extra cost of sending goods all round by Tweedmouth and Coldstream. Surely, the Company will be able to remedy this soon.'

NEW CORN MARKET? 28 January 1888

'Sir, One often hears the question asked – "How does the new railway affect Alnwick?" To this there are many replies. Certain businesses have necessarily suffered, whilst others have improved. One thing however is certain, and it is this: if tradesmen in Alnwick wish to reap the full advantage the new line is capable of affording, they must throw aside all petty jealousies and dislikes, which in the past have prevented them from working in union for the good of the town, and resolve to work together in a determined manner to establish a good corn market in Alnwick.'

'The question is one of the greatest importance, and I make bold to say that on its solution will depend in a great measure the fate of Alnwick commerce. – Yours, Progress'

13 February 1888

'At a public meeting held in the Town Hall, Mr. Crisp said it must be perfectly plain to everyone who had attended Alnwick corn market for many years that it had been gradually declining. That crisis they all saw had come about on the completion of the new railway...'

'Mr. Scott said it had an adverse effect to what many of them expected. If there had been a good corn market in Alnwick, the railway would have brought people from the west and the north, but as there did not happen to be a good corn market there, the railway instead of bringing the people to Alnwick, carried them to Berwick....'

MORE TRAINS? 4 May 1888

'Yesterday afternoon, a deputation from Alnwick and the north-western portion of Northumberland waited upon the Directors of the North-Eastern Railway Company, at Alnwick, to urge them to provide additional services for the district. The deputation suggested that an additional train should be run from the north on the Alnwick and Cornhill line, and arrive at Alnwick between 11 and 12 o'clock. It was also suggested that a refreshment room should be provided at Alnwick Railway Station. The Directors promised to consider the requests of the deputation.' A passenger train was scheduled to arrive just after mid-day (see Chapter 7), and a refreshment room was provided in the north-west corner of the station.

TOURISM: 5 May 1888

'The programme of the "Circular Pleasure Tours" of the North-Eastern Railway is just issued for the coming summer season. Some of the routes are made to include the Alnwick and Cornhill district, and we may expect to see a largely increased traffic set in towards this attractive part of the North.'

HEALTH RESORT WITH DONKEYS? 26 May 1888

'Wooler, now brought into convenient touch with the outside world promises to become very popular. The holiday seeker who once reclines on the Cheviot's grassy slopes, inhaling the fresh and invigorating breezes, and viewing the fascinating panorama beneath his feet, at once exclaims, "What a glorious place for the seeker after health; why should not Wooler become a second Malvern?" It remains for the inhabitants to do all in their power to attract and provide accommodation for visitors. The crowded station throughout last glorious Whit-Monday, showed plainly enough that people were beginning to find out that Wooler was a capital place at which to spend a holiday. A few climbing donkeys would not be at all a bad speculation for some enterprising inhabitant.'

NO EXCURSION TRAINS: 3 June 1888

'It was hoped that when we got the railway, we should have had large numbers of excursions visiting us. And so far, there has not been one excursion coming to Wooler, although we understand several applications have been made for such, and have been refused.... Would it be advisable for a public meeting to be called for at once, otherwise the season will be passed before any benefit is derived from the long looked-for railway.'

Nothing can have happened as on 28 July 1888: 'There was continued dissatisfaction at Wooler due to the failure to obtain excursions.' Half-day excursions were reported as running between Newcastle and Wooler in 1902.

LAST MAIL COACH IN NORTHUMBERLAND: 23 October 1888

'Active measures are being made by the numerous friends of Mr. Luke Reid in Wooler and vicinity to make a presentation in recognition of his long and valued service as mail coach driver between Wooler and Alnwick.' [6]

IGNORED BY THE MONSTER L&NWR: 8 December 1888

'A letter was received by a firm in Alnwick the other day from the London and North Western Railway Co. about a basket addressed to Ilderton Station, Alnwick and Cornhill Railway. This interesting document declared that there was no such station in existence, and that Alnwick was the nearest. So the poor little Alnwick and Cornhill is quite ignored by the monster L&NWR.'

STATION GARDENS COMPETITION: 30 March 1889

'The Directors of the Company residing in the northern portion of the system have agreed to offer prizes to station masters for the best display of plants and shrubs at the respective stations in their charge. The stations from Carlisle to Kelso and all the branch lines between these stations have been divided into four groups, and first and second prizes of £2 and £1 respectively will be awarded. The four groups are: 1) Main-Line stations between Manors and Tweedmouth; 2) Newcastle to Hexham [Carlisle?]; 3) St. Peter's to Jesmond, the Tynemouth and Riverside branches, Blyth and Tyne Line, and the Amble Branch; 4) the Kelso Branch and Alnwick and Cornhill Line.' See Chapter 8 for further details.

ROYAL VISIT: 16 July 1906

'Never before has there been such a vast assemblage of people in Alnwick at any one time as on Tuesday afternoon [10 July] when their Majesties the King and Queen paid a visit for the first time to our ancient and historic town. Not since the days of King Edward II has an English monarch slept in the State Rooms of Alnwick Castle.'

'The North-Eastern Railway Company as well as the town authorities had risen to the occasion of welcoming their Majesties in the way of decoration. On the Cornhill platform, an enclosure of gold and red cloth hung with evergreen and white flowers, had been erected where the Royal train was to be drawn up. Midway between this and the other platform, a perfect bower of plants and foliage, geraniums, begonias, primulas, fuschias, palms and ferns in variety had been formed, with a large Union Jack; and set in trellis, the word "WELCOME" as a background.'

'Stretching along the walls from here to the station exit were strings of evergreens and flowers, and descending from the roof, baskets of flowers in a variety of colours. At the point where the carriageway joins the main road, there appeared, "NORTHUMBRIA'S WELCOME" displayed on an arch of trellis work which was supported from either side by Venetian masts bearing flags and shields. At the bottom of the passenger entrance to the station were exhibited on a similar arch of fretwork the words, "LONG LIVE OUR KING AND QUEEN". This was the Railway Company's scheme, and it was greatly admired. The arrangements at the station were in the capable hands Mr. J. E. Carlisle, station master, and Inspector Rollinson of the North-Eastern Railway Police.'

'An extra train from Coldstream and Wooler brought large numbers of visitors, but was insufficient to pick up all the passengers desiring to travel from Hedgeley, Glanton and Whittingham, being so heavily loaded from the stations lying beyond. Rather than being deprived of seeing their Majesties, a good many, both men and women, set off and walked the eight miles to Alnwick....'

'At Wooler, where the whole of the tickets had been taken up by mid-day, something like one hundred more people intending going were not able to do so. The return journey was very tedious as the engine struck [sic] before reaching Summit, and further assistance had to be had from Alnwick. It was 10-0pm before the train reached Wooler.'

'The Royal Train was of the most luxurious description, and Mr. Worsdell, Chief Mechanical Engineer, was on the engine with Driver G. Thompson and Fireman Coates of Gateshead. Passenger, locomotive and brake inspectors were on the train.'

It was reported that some people, who had been unable to get on the trains, had walked a total of 18 miles to see their Majesties.

STRIKES: 11 August 1911

'The trains ran fairly well to and from Wooler all through the crisis, although there was some uncertainty as to the times of their departure and arrival. Tradesmen suffered some inconvenience through not being able to get supplies forward. A number of visitors had to prolong their stay while others were prevented from arriving. The *Gazette* newspaper had to be delivered by motor service.'

'The North Eastern Railwaymen were only on strike in sympathy with their brother workers as they already had what the others were fighting for. The settlement of the strike did not include the NER which was not a party to the agreement being signed.' [This totally unjustified action did nothing to further labour relations on the NER as the company had been the most advanced in the country in this field (the York Newcastle & Berwick Railway had negotiated with a 'men's representative' as early as 1849). The directors took this strike as a slap in the face.]

4 October 1919

'The unavailability of trains on the Alnwick and Cornhill line resulted in the weekly sale of fat stock at Wooler to be held on the previous Saturday in order to allow more time for the cattle to be walked to Newcastle, and 91 sheep to the Government slaughter house at Tweedmouth.'

17 October 1919

'On Tuesday afternoon, it was quite a pleasant sight to see a loco. puffing and moving at a crawling pace down the Cornhill line near Greensfield [Alnwick], with fourteen laden cattle waggons behind it. In going over the viaduct in the Waggon Way, the moo-cows were happy that the strike was over.'

## Route Available for Ramblers?

15 May 1953

'Will the track of the abandoned Alnwick to Ilderton railway line now in the process of being removed, ever become a permanent footpath for hikers and ramblers, perhaps with some topical name as *Elizabethan Way*?' [This was Coronation Year.]

'This question, which originated from a Tynemouth resident some time ago, has caught the public fancy, and some official bodies are showing interest. The subject, in fact, will be on the agenda of the next meeting of the Northumberland and North Durham Joint Standing Committee on Rights-of-Way, in Newcastle on May, 30th.'

'The Ramblers' Association is also enthusiastic. "The present suggestion has, we believe, precedents in other parts of the country, and the use of derelict railway lines as footpaths appears to be quite practicable. The use of the line, or a portion of it, would open out a stretch of country which is perhaps not too well supplied with through routes at present. To walk along it from Alnwick northwards would, from many points, provide fine and extensive views of our moorland country and hills, with the Cheviot itself as a centrepiece"'.

Unfortunately, although the idea had already been voiced in no less newspaper than *The Times* (13 March 1953) nothing was done. Whether the failure was due to objections by the adjacent landowners, lack of support by the local authorities or just being ahead of its time is not known. A decade later other counties, notably Durham, enthusiastically pursued the conversion of old railway formations into bridleways.

ON ALNWICK MOOR: SUGGESTED RAILWAY FOOTPATH

The branch railway line between Alnwick and Ilderton, Northumberland, is to be closed and the permanent way taken up. This view shows the part of the line as it ascends the western side of Alnwick Moor. It has been suggested in a letter to *The Times* that as "the doomed line follows a most beautiful and interesting route" it might well be formally established as a foot and bridle path and as an extension to the Pennine Way.

**Plate 11.6: a cutting from *The Times* for 13 March 1953 advocating the conversion of the southern end of the track-bed into a footpath.**

## ENDNOTES

1. The bridge over the River Ness, built by Meakin in 1862, collapsed due to scour on 7 Feb. 1989, cutting off rail access to the North of Scotland for several months.
2. Traffic Committee 4 October 1888.
3. NER *Loads of Engines* January 1911 and April 1917, Freight Train Timings 1911 and Working Timetables. The Working Timetables give 20 minutes as opposed to the Freight Train Timings of 30 minutes.
4. Another version says it was the double-headed express that caused the damage, but at least the date agrees.
5. Details from the Train Registers and interviews with some of those involved in the incident.
6. The NER had been offered this mail contract by the GPO for £50 per annum in March 1888, per Traffic Committee 3 April 1888.

**Plate 11.7: the last passenger train to Wooler was a Stephenson Locomotive Society special on 14 April 1963 hauled by Ivatt class 2MT No. 46474. J. M. Fleming.**

**APPENDICES**

**APPENDIX 1**

**MILES AND CHAINS FOR THE STATIONS AND SIGNAL CABINS ON THE LINE**

| M. Chs. | FEATURE |
|---------|---------|
| 0-00 | 'Coldstream West' (12m-44.33c on Tweedmouth to Kelso Branch) |
| 2-46.83 | *'Hagg' signal cabin – up side |
| 3-42.37 | 'Mindrum' signal cabin – down side |
| 3-44.86 | MINDRUM station D. P. |
| 4-78.48 | *'Langham Bridge' signal cabin – up side |
| 5-52.57 | *'Kilham Sidings' signal cabin – up side |
| 7-76.31 | KIRKNEWTON station D. P. |
| 7-76.92 | 'Kirknewton' signal cabin – down side |
| 8-24.42 | *'Kirknewton Crossing' signal cabin – up side |
| 9-57.84 | *'Yeavering' signal cabin – up side |
| 10-71.87 | AKELD station D.P. |
| 10-73.49 | 'Akeld' signal cabin – up side |
| 11-36.70 | *'Bendor' signal cabin – up side |
| 13-36.24 | *'Wooler North' signal cabin – up side |
| 13-41.89 | WOOLER station D.P. |
| 13-53.88 | *'Wooler South' signal cabin – up side |
| 13-75.99 | *'Brewery Road' signal cabin – up side |
| 15-8.32 | *'Wooler Haugh' [Haugh Head] signal cabin –up side |
| 17-6.89 | ILDERTON station D.P. |
| 17-9.6 | 'Ilderton' signal cabin – up side |
| 18-64.44 | *'Roseden' signal cabin – up side |
| 20-0.53 | WOOPERTON station D.P. |
| 20-2.51 | 'Wooperton' signal cabin – up side |
| 22-13.49 | *'Hedgeley' signal cabin - up side |
| 22-16.41 | HEDGELEY station D.P. |
| 24-14.66 | GLANTON station D.P. |
| 24-16.66 | 'Glanton' signal cabin - up side |
| 25-69.66 | 'Whittingham' signal cabin – up side |
| 25-70.87 | WHITTINGHAM station D.P. |
| 25-78.15 | 'Saw Mill Siding' ground frame 1917 – down side. |
| 27-16.76 | **Commencement of Tunnel** |
| 27-32.73 | **Termination of Tunnel** |
| 28-62.08 | 'Edlingham' signal cabin - up side |
| 28-64.11 | EDLINGHAM station D.P. |
| 30-52.90 | 'Frazer's Siding' ground frame 1916-1919 – down side |
| 31-36.59 | 'Summit' signal cabin –up side |
| 35-32.40 | 'Alnwick North' signal cabin –up side |
| 35-46.42 | **Termination of branch at Alnwick Station Junction** |

**\* indicates signal cabin controlling a level crossing**

**NOTES:**
There are 80 chains of 22 yards to 1 mile. The D.P. is the mileage of the centre of the station from which all fares and rates are charged. As early as 1901 the signal boxes at Mindrum, Akeld, Wooperton, Glanton and Edlingham were replaced by dwarf frames housed in an extension to the station verandah, but the mileages given are for the original cabins and not the dwarf frames.

## APPENDIX 2

**The NER table of 1912 for equating smaller animals to fully grown cattle**

|  | EQUIVALENT | | | |
|---|---|---|---|---|
| CATTLE | 1 | 2 | 3 | 4 |
| PONIES UP TO 12 HANDS | 1 | 2 | 3 | 4 |
| SHEEP OR GOATS | 3 | 7 | 11 | 15 |
| LAMBS | 5 | 10 | 15 | 20 |
| CALVES UP TO 12 MONTHS | 2 | 5 | 7 | 10 |
| PIGS | 3 | 6 | 9 | 12 |

## APPENDIX 3

1913 rates for parcels between NER and non-competitive stations irrespective of distance.

| Parcels | Weight | Cost |
|---|---|---|
| Weight not exceeding | 2lbs | 4d |
| Weight not exceeding | 3lbs | 5d |
| Above 3lbs up to 14lbs |  | 6d |

## APPENDIX 4

**Station Masters appointed in 1887.**

**Edlingham**; H. Harrison, formerly a signalman at Alnwick. **Whittingham**; T. Newton, formerly S. M. at Howden. **Glanton**; W. Cornforth formerly S. M. at Aldin Grange. **Hedgeley**; J. Forster formerly booking clerk at Alnwick. **Wooperton**; H. Hollamby. **Ilderton**; W. Bird, formerly senior clerk at Alnwick. **Wooler**; J. Aitchison. **Akeld**; T. Edgar. **Kirknewton**; B. Wright. **Mindrum**; J. Storey.

## APPENDIX 5

**Classes of locomotives used on the line: -**

NER Tender Classes: 38, 59, 398, 901, 'Tennants', 1440, 1463, C, P1, P3, F, M, Q, R, S1 and S2.
NER Tank Classes: BTP, 8, A, B, E, O and U.
Ex Hull & Barnsley Classes (post 1923): J23 and J28.
Ex NBR Classes (post 1923): J35, J36 and J37.
LNER Classes: A3, D49, J39, V1 and V2.
Other Types: WD 2-8-0, LMS and BR designed moguls.

The locomotives were supplied by Alnmouth or Tweedmouth sheds. North Eastern locomotives known to have been used prior to the removal of the passenger service were: - BTP class No. 199, class A No. 483, class B No. 857, class M Nos. 1621 and 1625.

*Rear cover: a poster by Grainger Johnson printed soon after the First World War somewhat exaggerates the features of the line near Edlingham, and makes an interesting comparison with David Sutcliffe's painting on the front cover. Private collection.*